A COMMENTARY

LET'S TALK ABOUT
The Book of
ROMANS

DR. MELVIN H. KING

ZYIA CONSULTING
Illuminate & Transcend

Let's Talk About The Book of Romans: A Commentary

Copyright © 2022 by Dr. Melvin H. King

To contact the author, email pastormhking@ddm-inc.org.

All rights reserved. No portion of this book may be reproduced, stored in a retrieval system, or transmitted in any form or by any means—electronic, mechanical, photocopy, recording, scanning, or other—except for brief quotations in critical reviews or articles, without the prior written permission of the publisher.

Zyia Consulting
Book Writing & Publishing Company
www.nyishaddavis.com
nyisha.d.davis@gmail.com

Unless otherwise noted, all Scripture quotations are taken from www.biblestudytools.com; GOD's Word Translation (GW) or New King James Version.

Cover Design: Zyia Consulting, LLC

Cover Image Credit: Love You Stock (Shutterstock.com)

ISBN: 9780578357218

Printed in the United States of America.

Dr. Melvin H. King

Pastor Melvin H. King knows the power of influence and understands the importance of walking out GOD's plan for his life by Faith. As a native of Atlanta, Georgia, born to Melvin & Christine King, integrity, persistence, and a love for GOD was instilled in him. He was taught the importance of having the ability to empower oneself by keeping GOD at the center of his life at all times. He is no stranger to hearing the voice of GOD. For at the young age of twelve, he began his journey when he received his calling into the ministry. Not quite understanding the fullness of that call, Pastor King knew, one day, that GOD the HOLY SPIRIT, would give him a clear and measurable vision of how GOD, the Father, desired to use him in the work of the ministry.

After graduating from C.L. Harper High School, Pastor King continued to further his education at Tuskegee University in Alabama, where he studied Architecture. While in attendance at Tuskegee University, he served as Executive Committee Director of the Student Government Association (S.G.A.). Where he was responsible for all freshmen activities. He later continued his educational pursuits at Clayton State College, where he enrolled in the Architectural program. In 1990, Pastor King entered into the International Brotherhood of Electrical Workers (I.B.E.W.) program; completing studies toward becoming an Electrician, and became a certified Electrician in 1996.

Although Pastor King was pursuing his education, he never forgot the day that GOD called him. By the age of twenty-one, GOD the HOLY SPIRIT gave him the understanding that he needed. Pastor King responded by accepting his calling into the ministry. Under the tutelage, guidance, and leadership of Bishop Dreyfus C. Smith, Pastor of Wings of Faith Ministries in Atlanta, Georgia, Pastor King walked into the beginning of his life as a minister of JESUS CHRIST, our Savior. He later received his license to minister the Gospel on December 10, 1989, and was later ordained in October 1994.

In August 1991, as Pastor King continued his journey being led by the SPIRIT of GOD, he moved to Los Angeles, California, where he served in the ministry under the late Dr. J.W. Evans, his uncle. Pastor King then enrolled into La Verne University School of Theology. He later obtained a degree and a Baccalaureate Certificate in Christian Ministry, both from The King's University, founded by Pastor Jack Hayford. Pastor King completed post-graduate studies at Oxford University in Oxford, England in 2009.

On January 11, 1998, Pastor King was elected the Pastor of the Mary Magdalene Missionary Baptist Church in Los Angeles, California. He was installed on March 1, 1998. Under his leadership at Mary Magdalene, over 4,000 souls surrendered their lives to Christ. Two years later, on October 26, 2000, his accomplishments continued, and he became a member of the Macedonia International Fellowship under the leadership and guidance of Bishop Kenneth C. Ulmer, in Johannesburg, South Africa, in an association of pastors representing ministries in South Africa and the U.S.A.

While holding steadfast to the Word of GOD and the values that his parents taught him, Pastor King, remaining firm on his promise to GOD to not compromise His Word, stepped out by Faith and resigned as Pastor of Mary Magdalene. GOD honored his Faithfulness and on October 10, 2010, Divine Deliverance Ministries (10D/10D/10M) was birthed. The ministry at DDM continues to grow strong as it holds on to the mission of spreading the Gospel to the ends of the world, and inviting others to become new Disciples of JESUS CHRIST.

On April 18, 2015, Pastor King received his Doctorate of Divinity degree from Saint Thomas Christian University, and is acknowledged as a visionary, with the ability to preach and teach the Word of GOD with simplicity and accuracy. Pastor King is noted for his upbeat, enthusiastic style as he continues to dynamically lead others into the "Next Dimension" of their journey in CHRIST, just as he has. He remains committed to restoring the Kingdom of GOD, preaching the Gospel and lifting up the name of JESUS!

Pastor King additional career highlights:

- Featured three times on the television talk show "Oh Drama!"
- Appeared on the television show "Raising Whitley" broadcasted by the Oprah Winfrey Network (OWN).
- Produced a nationally televised ministry on the BET Network.
- 2004 received a Certificate of Recognition of Completion from The Los Angeles Division of the FBI Citizens' Academy.
- 2014 received The Senior Pastor Institute Certificate of Completion from Dr. R.A. Vernon.

Table of Contents

Introduction to the Book of Romans 9

Chapter 1: Paul the Servant 12
- The Greeting: Verses 1-7
- Paul's Prayer & Desire to Visit Rome: Verses 8-17
- GOD's Anger Against Sinful Humanity: Verses 18-32

Chapter 2: Hear, Believe & Obey 26
- GOD Will Judge Everyone: Verses 1-13
- GOD Will Judge People Who Are Not Jewish: Verses 14-29

Chapter 3: We All Fall Short 39
- Everyone Is a Sinner: Verses 1-20
- GOD Gives Us HIS Approval as a Gift: Verses 21-31

Chapter 4: We Have GOD's Approval by Faith 50

Chapter 5: At Peace With GOD 60
- We Are at Peace With God, Because of JESUS: Verses 1-11
- A Comparison Between Adam & CHRIST: Verses 12-21

Chapter 6: No Longer Slaves 73
- No Longer Slaves to Sin, but GOD's Servants: Verses 1-23

Chapter 7: Moses' Law 83
- The Reality of The Law & The Flesh: Verses 1-6
- Moses' Laws Show What Sin Is: Verses 7-13
- GOD's Standards Are at War With Sin's Standards: Verses 14-25

Chapter 8: GOD's SPIRIT 95
- GOD's SPIRIT Makes Us HIS Children: Verses 1-17
- GOD's SPIRIT Helps Us: Verses 18-27
- Nothing Can Separate Us from GOD's Love: Verses 28-39

Chapter 9: Paul's Concerns 109
- Paul's Concern for the Jewish People: Verses 1-23
- GOD Chose People Who Are Not Jewish: Verses 24-33

Chapter 10: Just Believe 120
- If You Believe, You Will Be Saved: Verses 1-21

Chapter 11: GOD's Continous Love 131

RECAP 143

Chapter 12: A Life Dedicated to GOD 145
- Dedicate Your Lives to God: Verses 1-29

Chapter 13: The Government & Love One Another 154
- Obey the Government, Verses 1-6
- Love One Another, Verses 7-14

Chapter 14: Strengthen the Weak 164
- How to Treat Christians Who Are Weak in Faith: Verses 1-22

Chapter 15: Unity & Paul's Desire 174
- God Gives Us Unity: Verses 1-13
- Paul's Desire to Tell the Good News to the World: Verses 14-33

Chapter 16: Paul's Farewell 188

Introduction to the Book of Romans

When the Apostle Paul wrote his letter to the Christian Believers in Rome, his purpose in writing to the Romans appears to have been to answer the unbelieving. His focus was to teach the believing Jew, confirm the Christians, convert the Gentile, and show that the Gentile converts are equal with the Jew. Even though Paul didn't establish a church or met most of the Believers in Rome, he had heard that the Believers there were growing in their faith. He was convinced that the Believers in Rome would continue his work of taking the Gospel of JESUS CHRIST to the Roman empire.

While in the city of Corinth, Paul wanted to encourage and teach the Christian Believers in Rome. That was the purpose of him writing this letter to the Roman Christian Believers. His message to them was the way of a sinner's acceptance of GOD, or justification is merely by grace through faith in the righteousness of CHRIST without distinction of nations. The main theme of Romans is that righteousness comes as a gift of GOD and is receivable by faith alone.

The Judaizing Christians were trying to make the acceptance of GOD a mixture of The Law and The Gospel. They were trying to shut out the Gentiles from sharing in the blessings of salvation that was done by JESUS CHRIST. Paul urges the Romans not to return to their old human nature, but to live free from sin and death through the power of the HOLY SPIRIT. (8:10-11)

The Book of Romans is a very good book to study. It contains almost every Christian doctrine in some form. It is considered Paul's most important epistle. It doesn't just tell us what the Christian life is all about, but it also tells us how we should live as Believers. It tells us what to believe, how we should behave, what our faith is all about and gives us GOD's solution to our sin problem.

The fact that GOD is a GOD of wrath bothers a lot of people. Even including some Christian Believers. Yes, GOD is a GOD of love, but HE is also a GOD who cannot and will not tolerate sin and evil. That's why Paul places emphasis on GOD's infinite power and how the message of JESUS CHRIST can change the sinner's life. GOD is saying to us in this letter, "I love you. And, because I love you, I don't want you to live a life of sin and evil that will bring destruction."

Even though GOD loves us, HIS love has given us freewill. HE will not control our choices. You can't choose to live in sin and evil and avoid the consequences of your choices. GOD does not hate anyone for their choices. But, HE will never remove our free will or the consequence of our choices.

During the time Paul wrote this letter, a lot of Believers were considering themselves righteous and everyone else unrighteous. He tells the Believers, "We can't judge others, because there are some sins we also commit." In Romans 2:1 Paul says to them, *You, therefore, have no excuse, you who pass judgment on someone else, for at whatever point you judge the other, you are condemning yourself, because you who pass judgment do the same things.*

As Believers, even though we have been saved and delivered, we should never see ourselves as more righteous than anyone. If we commit hatred, gossip, slander, or deception, we can't judge someone involved in homosexuality or adultery. GOD has judged us all to be equally guilty. Romans 3:23 lets us know that *all have sinned*. And, because *all have sinned*, then all of us are in need of a redeemer. Everyone needs GOD's grace. The grace of GOD is ready to rescue and redeem us. We are going to see Paul talk about this in chapter 4.

As a matter of fact, he gives us three stages of redemption: Justification, Sanctification, and Glorification. Justification is us standing before GOD as if we have never sinned. When we are justified, we are delivered from the penalty of sin. Righteousness can't be earned. We only become righteous when we choose to accept the gift of GOD in JESUS CHRIST.

When we are sanctified, we dedicate ourselves to GOD. To be sanctified means to be 'set apart for GOD'. That's why true Believers are called saints. We are set apart for HIS service. When you have been set apart for HIS service, you are free and no longer in bondage to sin. The book of Galatians taught us you can't be in bondage to something you have been freed from. If you are in bondage to something you have been freed from, your bondage is a choice. We have been redeemed. We have been bought with a price.

When it comes to glorification, the most important thing you can do with your life is to give yourself to GOD and to live for HIM. I don't know about you, but I want my life to bring glory to GOD and not shame. The way we bring glory to GOD is by presenting our bodies as living sacrifices. (Romans 12:1) Presenting our bodies not only brings glory to GOD, but it also affects our lives; your attitude toward others changes, and you feel a desire to reach those who are lost that choose to live in sin and evil. When you have experienced justification, sanctification, and glorification, you want others to experience it for themselves as well.

I don't have time to put your lifestyle under a microscope. I want you to experience GOD's love and power for yourself. That was Paul's message to the Christian Believers in Rome. "Don't take what GOD has done for you and look down on other people. Realize that the same GOD that saved you must be the same GOD that has to save them. Just like you needed grace to step in for you, realize they also need grace to step in for them."

Knowing that GOD is a GOD of love and a GOD of wrath, I want everyone to experience HIS love instead of their choices causing them to experience HIS wrath. In Romans 1:32 Paul says, *Although they know the righteous judgment of GOD and those who do such things deserve to die, they not only do these things but also approve of others who do them.* If GOD didn't love us, HE would have never come in the flesh and died in the flesh for us. The righteous ONE died on behalf of the unrighteous. Therefore, GOD doesn't send anyone to hell. Their free will to *do these things* and their corrupted nature do.

Remember, love is GOD giving you the absolute right to choose your course of action. Love is also GOD giving you the perfect freedom to live with the consequences of your actions. Now, let's talk about the Book of Romans.

Chapter 1
Paul the Servant

Greeting
Verses 1-7

It is said that Paul may have been in the city of Corinth when he wrote this letter to the Roman. Paul did not think he would ever have the opportunity to visit Rome. Even though he had a great desire to go there. So, he decided to write the Believers this letter. He wrote the book of Romans, because he wanted to reveal a vision he had about the Roman Christian Believers. Since he didn't establish the churches in Rome, we find Paul trying to make himself familiar with the Believers in this letter.

The good thing about the Believers in Rome, when Paul visited other cities and when he would establish a church in that city, that church was mostly built on the message of CHRIST and also signs and miracles. The church in Rome was built primarily on belief. The message of CHRIST got to Rome. And the moment it got there, it spread like wildfire.

With Rome being the superpower, Paul also knew that preaching in Rome was a great platform to spread the message about JESUS. When it came to the Believers in Rome, Paul had a special love for them. When Paul was brought to Rome as a prisoner, the citizens of Rome treated Paul with kindness. (Acts 27)

In Romans 1:1, this is considered to be Paul's greeting to the Roman Believers. *From Paul, a servant of JESUS CHRIST, called to be an apostle and appointed to spread the Good News of GOD.* What did you notice about verse 1? First, he calls himself a servant. Second, he presents his title. Then third, he informs them of his assignment. Paul could have very easily just focused on his position as an apostle. The first thing Paul presented himself as was a servant. If this had been today, the only thing you would have gotten was their title. When you present your title first, what you're saying is, "I want you to respect me, because of my title. And, because of my title, there's a certain treatment that I am expecting from you."

The reason a lot of people present their title first is because they want to be treated according to their title, and not because of the assignment they have been called to do. The danger of getting caught up in your title first is, it makes you lose focus on your assignment. What good does it do you to have a title when you don't know your assignment?

Paul says, "I'm a servant first. Don't get caught up in my title. I'm here on assignment." Not only does Paul tell them that he's a servant, but he also informs them of who it is he serves. "I'm a servant of JESUS CHRIST. Called by CHRIST to be an apostle. If I was called by CHRIST, I am required to serve the one that has called me." My question is, how can anyone get caught up in their title and not be willing to serve the one that called them?

If you're not serving CHRIST, my question would be, bishop, minister, preacher, who called you? Surely, you don't have a problem serving, especially when GOD is the one that has called you. Your title shouldn't cause you to work less, but it should cause you to serve more. Paul said, "I'm a servant first! Called to be an Apostle. Appointed to spread the Gospel." The moment I accepted JESUS as my Savior, I became a servant. After I became a servant, GOD called me to Pastor. HIM calling me to be a Pastor does not stop me from being a servant. I'm a servant first. Called to Pastor GOD's people.

Question. Why is it in the church, the moment we get a title, we stop serving? Or the more titles we get, the less we serve? I have had ministers who were doing a great job as regular disciples. The moment they received a title, I couldn't get them to serve. How can someone be called by GOD to minister and serve HIS people, and they are not willing to serve HIS people?

In verses 2-7, Paul says, "Here's what I was appointed to do." *(GOD had already promised this Good News through his prophets in the Holy Scriptures. This Good News is about HIS Son, our Lord JESUS CHRIST. In HIS human nature, HE was a descendant of David. In HIS spiritual, holy nature HE was declared the Son of GOD. This was shown in a powerful way when HE came back to life. Through HIM we have received GOD's kindness and the privilege of being apostles who bring people from every nation to the obedience that is associated with faith. This is for the honor of HIS name. You are among those who have been called to belong to JESUS CHRIST.) To everyone in Rome whom GOD loves and has called to be HIS holy people. Goodwill and peace from GOD our Father and the Lord JESUS CHRIST are yours!*

Look who's talking, Paul. The same one that used to persecute Christian Believers. The same one that would hunt Christian Believers down. But, because of his experience on Damascus Road, he's now the biggest advocate for JESUS. Before we license anyone else to preach, I think we should ask them about their Damascus experience. It's hard to have a Damascus experience, and not be faithful to your call. It's impossible to be appointed by GOD to do an assignment and not do it! To be called by GOD and not do your assignment is telling HIM 'No'. I would understand if I called you to preach and you told me 'No'. If GOD has called you and appointed you, how do you tell GOD, 'No'?

That's why I think a Damascus Road experience is needed. Only a Damascus experience can take someone like Paul, who was mean, brutal, ruthless, and cold-blooded, and turn them into a spiritual, kind, compassionate, kindhearted person. Look at how Paul is talking in verse 7. To everyone in Rome, GOD loves you and has called you to be HIS holy people. Goodwill and peace from GOD to you, my brother. Does that mean that people who are still mean, hateful, and evil haven't had a Damascus experience? What would turn a cold-blooded killer into an evangelist? An experience with JESUS on Damascus Road. When you have had a true experience, you don't have to question your call. That's why the saying says, "some were sent and some just went." You can always tell the ones who just went, because it's hard to get them to serve.

Paul says in verse 5, Through HIM we have received grace and apostleship for obedience to the faith among all nations for His name. WOW! If I can't be obedient to the faith, I have not been called at all. The text says Through HIM. HIM who? The ONE that has called us. HE has given me grace to help me be obedient to the faith. If I can't be obedient to the faith, I have not been called. I'm just disobedient. Disobedience translates to defiance. Which translates to rebellion. How can someone be called and refused to serve? Either they weren't called, or they are just being disobedient.

Paul's Prayer and Desire to Visit Rome
Verses 8-17

In verse 10, we see Paul expressing his desire to visit Rome. Keep in mind, when Paul wrote the book of Romans to the Believers in Rome, it is said that Paul may have been in the city of Corinth. In verses 8-10. Paul says *First, I thank my GOD through JESUS CHRIST for every one of you because the news of your faith is spreading throughout the whole world. I serve GOD by spreading the Good News about HIS SON. GOD is my witness that I always mention you every time I pray. I ask that somehow GOD will now, at last, make it possible for me to visit you.*

Not only do we see that Paul had a strong desire to visit the Believers in Rome, but the news about the Believers in Rome is spreading all over the world. Question. What would make this church in Rome so popular? In other words, what were the Believers doing to make them known all over the world? They were living the life they witnessed, they showed a passion for what they believed, and they didn't mind proclaiming to the world what they believe.

In other words, they had a "Halal" spirit. Whereby they didn't mind boasting about GOD. Not only did they have a "Halal" spirit, but they also had a "Yada" spirit whereby they did not mind boasting about GOD in public. Since they didn't mind boasting about their GOD in public, people heard their message. People heard their testimony all over the world. The reason people aren't running to the Church is that the Church is afraid to boast about GOD in public. We don't want to offend anyone. Instead of boasting about our faith, we keep silent about our faith. Instead of standing on our faith, we alter and compromise the truth of what we believe just so we can be accepted by those who don't believe.

We want to be politically correct rather than to be spiritually obedient. The reason prayer was taken out of the schools is because the Believers were too afraid to boast about GOD in public. Whenever the Believers stop boasting about GOD in public, sin runs rampant. Why? *At the name of JESUS every knee shall bow, and every tongue shall confess that HE is Lord.* (Philippians 2:10-11)

The problem in the Body of CHRIST is the Believers are too afraid to boast about JESUS' name in public. Do you want to know how to control sin in our society? Start boasting JESUS' name in public. It's hard to boast HIS name in public when we are also involved in the same sins the world is in. Boasting JESUS' name might bring exposure to our sin.

Do you know that certain Pastors purposely don't preach on certain matters due to their involvement in those matters? Whenever the pulpit is silent, the people struggle. In other words, whatever the pulpit refused to talk about, the people struggle in those areas. People live without morals. Whenever truth becomes silent, then sin dominates. No sin should feel comfortable sitting in a church where GOD's Word is going forth. You are to feel convicted every now and then. Show me a church where sin feels comfortable. I'll show you a place where the Word of GOD is not going forth. If sin feels comfortable, then GOD's presence is absent. That which is ungodly cannot feel comfortable around that which is holy.

The Roman Believers' faith became popular because they did not mind boasting about what they believed in public. In verses 11-12, Paul tells the Believers *I long to see you to share a spiritual blessing with you so that you will be strengthened. What I mean is that we may be encouraged by each other's faith.* There's a purpose for us coming together as Believers. What's the purpose? To strengthen each other.

Look at what Paul says in verses 13-15. *I want you to know, brothers and sisters, that I often planned to visit you. However, until now I have been kept from doing so. What I want is to enjoy some of the results of working among you as I have also enjoyed the results of working among the rest of the nations. I have an obligation to those who are civilized and those who aren't, to those who are wise and those who aren't. That's why I'm eager to tell you who live in Rome the Good News also.*

Not only are we supposed to share the Gospel of CHRIST with those who don't believe, but we are also supposed to share it with those who do believe. I might know something you don't know that you need to know. You might know something I don't know that I need to know. How many of you actually share the Gospel with other Believers?

When we see how ministry went forth back then and how different it is now, I see why the early Church exploded with new converts daily. People had a passion for The Gospel. Watch this, in a world whereby the Christian Believers were a minority, they had a passion to boast their belief publicly. Now that Christianity is the majority, now it's hard to get anyone to say anything openly. Why? Here's why, verse 16, *For I am not ashamed of the Gospel of CHRIST...* Stop! Do you think the reason people are no longer boasting about The Gospel publicly is that they are ashamed of The Gospel? Most people are silent on matters they are ashamed of. If I'm not ashamed of The Gospel, I should not mind boasting about it in public. Not only should I not be ashamed to boast what I believe publicly, but also boast what I believe politically.

Here's why. My political views should never alter what I believe. My belief should always alter my view which determines how I stand politically. Paul said, "I see y'all are a lot like me. You are not ashamed of The Gospel of JESUS CHRIST. And because you are not ashamed, you don't mind boasting. Since y'all don't mind boasting, the world gets to hear the message."

Verse 16 continues to say *for it is the power of GOD to salvation for everyone who believes, for the Jew first and also for the Greek.* The message about CHRIST has power. When we first became Believers, the Book of Acts tells us that GOD has given every Believer the power to be a witness. Acts 1:8 says *But you will receive power when the HOLY SPIRIT comes to you. Then you will be my witnesses to testify about me in Jerusalem, throughout Judea and Samaria, and to the ends of the earth.*

Watch how powerful verse 16 is, *it is GOD's power that will save everyone who believes.* All we must do as a Believer is to tell the message. If the person listening believes the message, GOD's power will turn around and save them. The problem in the Body of CHRIST is we don't have enough Believers that are willing to tell the message. How do we get visitors to come to Church? By boasting to someone publicly. If the disciples never say anything, then how are unbelievers ever supposed to come to CHRIST.

There's so much to be said about verse 17. *GOD's approval is revealed in this Good News. This approval begins and ends with faith as Scripture says, "The person who has GOD's approval will live by faith."* How do you tell a real Believer from a fake one? The one who GOD has approved lives by faith. Walk by faith. Once you truly believe the message of JESUS CHRIST, GOD takes that faith and counts it as righteousness. Therefore, making that person acceptable to GOD.

Watch this, sin cannot stand before GOD. What makes me able to stand before GOD? He takes my faith, that which I truly believe, and counts it as righteousness. Which causes me to be able to stand before GOD. Everyone that calls themselves a Believer, is not. The only way to tell true Believers is they walk by faith. They walk by what they say they believe. In other words, you can't call yourself a Believer and everything about your lifestyle contradicts what you say you believe. A person who truly believes lives by faith. GOD takes that faith and counts it as righteousness and acceptable.

GOD's Anger Against Sinful Humanity
Verses 18-32

    Paul was so clever in writing Romans chapter 1. He goes from talking about those who don't mind boasting about The Gospel, who are not ashamed of the Gospel and how GOD approves of them, to talking about those who GOD rejects. Verses 18 down to verse 32 deal with those who GOD rejects. We, in the Body of CHRIST, make it so hard to recognize true Believers when the evidence is black-and-white. Paul makes it so simple to recognize those who GOD approves and those who GOD rejects. Look at how he just comes out in verse 18. *GOD's anger is revealed from heaven against every ungodly and immoral thing people do as they try to suppress the truth by their immoral living.* To back up verse 18, Paul says in verse 19 *What can be known about GOD is clear to them because HE has made it clear to them.*

    It's no way to be a true Believer and continue to live in sin. You can never use the excuse "I didn't know." Verse 19 says everything you need to know about GOD has been made clear. If someone is living in sin, continually practicing sin, it's because they are choosing to live in that lifestyle. All these excuses that we are choosing to accept in the Body of CHRIST, Paul said, "There is no excuse for living in sin and living ungodly. The truth has already been made known to you." Not only has it been made known, but look at what the text says, what was made known to them, it manifested in them.

    To live ungodly, I must literally refuse to live right. There can't be an excuse, because I have to say, "Here's the truth which has been made known to me, and here's what I want to do." Am I going to tell Truth? No, because

I'm choosing to do what I want to do. The moment we are exposed to the Truth, according to the text, it should manifest through us.

Verse 18 says they hold the truth in unrighteousness. Every time someone chooses to live in sin after Truth has been made known, they 'hold' the Truth in the midst of the sin they are committing. Wow! That's deep. That's like committing fornication with the Bible in your hand. Do y'all really understand how powerful grace and mercy are? To step in and save us and even protect us while we are standing in sin holding on to GOD's truth.

Paul starts to explain how all of this happened in verses 20-23, *From the creation of the world, GOD's invisible qualities, HIS eternal power, and divine nature, have been clearly observed in what HE made. As a result, people have no excuse. They knew GOD but did not praise and thank HIM for being GOD. Instead, their thoughts were pointless, and their misguided minds were plunged into darkness. While claiming to be wise, they became fools. They exchanged the glory of the immortal GOD for statues that looked like mortal humans, birds, animals, and snakes.*

They did all this while being aware of GOD's truths. Look at verse 23 again. They traded GOD in for statues, knowing who GOD is. Question. How do you trade GOD in for a statute? The text says the statues looked like *mortal humans, birds, animals and snakes*. This is what they traded GOD in for back then. What are some of the things we trade GOD in for today? Anything we put before GOD, especially knowing who GOD is, becomes our statute.

- Some people's jobs are their statute.
- Some people's relationships are their statute.
- Some people's success is their statue.

Why? They longer feel they need GOD. Because they replaced GOD for statues, look at what verse 24 says. *For this reason GOD allowed their lusts to control them.* Wow! Can you imagine GOD allowing your lust to control you? *As a result, they dishonor their bodies by sexual perversion with each other.* Whenever you have a flesh problem, it's because GOD has allowed your lust to have control of you. Whatever you put before GOD and make your priority, GOD allows that to take control of you.

Verse 25, *These people have exchanged GOD's truth for a lie. So, they have become ungodly and serve what is created rather than the Creator, who is blessed forever. Amen!* Did y'all just catch what Paul said at the end of verse 25? Paul said ungodly people have traded GOD in for something else. Only GOD is blessed forever. Whatever I have traded GOD for is only blessed for the moment. Only GOD is blessed forever. If I want to forever be blessed, I need to always make GOD my number one priority. That was powerful! Not my hustle, but my GOD!

Verses 26 and 27 are going to be a bit hard, but it's going to bring a lot of understanding. *For this reason GOD allowed their shameful passions to control them. Their women have exchanged natural sexual relations for unnatural ones. Likewise, their men have given up natural sexual relations with women and burn with lust for each other. Men commit indecent acts with men, so they experience among themselves the punishment they deserve for their perversion.*

When it comes to these verses, a lot of people like to say, this is a matter of interpretation. I think Paul makes this simple and plain. Paul says in these verses that you will know when someone has turned away from GOD; when they have taken natural sexual relations and traded them in for unnatural ones.

Notice what the text says. When women start having sexual relations with each other and men start having sexual relations with each other, it is perversion! According to the apostle Paul, one way to know when someone is totally disconnected from GOD is when they start practicing sexual perversions.

Because of these perversions, verse 27 says, they will experience *the punishment they deserve for their perversions*. Paul even goes into more detail in verse 28. *And because they thought it was worthless to acknowledge GOD, GOD allowed their own immoral minds to control them. So, they do these indecent things.*

Here's why it's a perversion to GOD. Not only does the problem lie in their flesh, but it also lies in their mind. We can try to clean it up, fix it up or even change it up. Paul is pretty clear regarding this issue. Paul says you will know them because of what verses 29 through 31 says *Their lives are filled with all kinds of sexual sins, wickedness, and greed. They are mean. They are filled with envy, murder, quarreling, deceit and viciousness. They are gossippers, slanderers, haters of GOD, haughty, arrogant and boastful. They think up new ways to be cruel. They don't obey their parents, don't have any sense, don't keep promises, and don't show love to their own families or mercy to others.*

If a person's life is filled with sexual perversion, wickedness, greed, hatred, jealousy, deceit, gossip, pride, and lies, how can they even fix their mouth to say that they are a Believer? Not only does Paul say they are not Believers, but look at what he says in verse 32. *Although they know GOD's judgment that those who do such things deserve to die, they not only do these things but also approve of others who do them.* Paul says, "Not only do you participate in these things, but you try to encourage other people to practice them."

So basically, misery loves company. As a Believer, I should never get too comfortable with any sin. Not only should I not get comfortable with sin, but even if I find myself having a problem with sin, I should never find myself encouraging other people to sin also. As a true Believer, one who believes GOD and HIS Word, I should always be leery of anyone who tries to encourage me to sin. Their invitation to sin is not showing me love or acceptance. It says to me they don't care about my soul. How can you love me and not care that those who do such things deserve to die?

Chapter 2
Hear, Believe & Obey

GOD Will Judge Everyone
Verses 1-13

Before we just hopped right into chapter 2, very quickly, let's make sure we understand what took place in chapter 1. I remember being on a talk show, and I was asked, "What does the church look like?" I responded, "The church doesn't have a look, it has a behavior." We have made the church look a certain type of way. When I responded to another question, "The Church is the Believers," I was then asked, "Well, what does that look like?" I responded, "It's not a look, it's a behavior. The behavior is never worldly."

The only effective way we can get the message of JESUS CHRIST to the world is, Believers cannot be ashamed to boast about the Gospel. The Believers must come out of their comfort zone and be willing to boast about CHRIST to the world; to the people on our jobs and to the people in our neighborhood. When the Believers in Rome boasted about the Gospel of JESUS CHRIST, the church exploded.

Believers are scared to boast about what they believe. For some reason or another, we are afraid of offending people with our beliefs. We are afraid of offending the unbeliever when it's the unbeliever that needs to be saved. Did y'all hear how crazy that sounded? We are afraid to boast about what we believe, so we don't offend the unbeliever when it's going to take what we believe for the unbeliever to be saved.

Our salvation shouldn't be a secret. It should be something we want to run and tell the world about. Could one of the reasons why a lot of people are afraid to express what they believe be because they want the freedom to live any kind of way they choose? They don't want to be held accountable for living right.

As a Believer, it should be easier to live right than it is to live wrong. Every time I do something wrong, it should disturb the GOD in me. If someone finds pleasure by constantly doing wrong, living in sin, and doing people wrong, then it's a strong possibility that GOD is not manifested in them. True Believers have GOD manifested in them according to Paul in Chapter 1:19.

It's not possible to have GOD in you and you are comfortable living in sin. You might be in sin, but you shouldn't be comfortable. GOD's truth is in you. If HIS truth is in you, it should convict you every time you go against HIS Truth. Why? Romans 1:18 told us how can you hold the Truth in unrighteousness and feel comfortable? You can't.

This now takes us into Romans chapter 2. It's kind of strange that Paul ends chapter 1 by talking about the sins of the unbeliever, then hops into chapter 2, talking about the dangers of judging. You would think Paul would present chapter 2 before chapter 1, but he starts off chapter 2 talking about judging. The reason is that Paul wants us to be able to identify the sins of the unbeliever, but not put ourselves in a position to judge the unbelievers because of their sins. So, he presents their sins first and then tells us not to judge.

When you put yourself in the position of a judge, it's hard for you to witness the message of CHRIST. You would be too busy being a judge. It's not our job to judge. It's our job to witness. Two different job descriptions. It's not our job to judge the unbeliever, it's our job to witness the message of JESUS CHRIST to them. Paul's purpose and mission in chapter 2 are, that even though GOD has taken our faith and made it the righteousness of HIMSELF, don't allow your righteousness to turn into self-righteousness. Our faith only makes us acceptable and presentable to GOD. It does not give us authority to judge and criticize unbelievers.

Verse 1 says *No matter who you are, if you judge anyone, you have no excuse. When you judge another person, you condemn yourself, since you, the judge, do the same things.* Paul is saying, this person has put themselves in the position of a judge. You can't be a servant if you have promoted yourself to the position of a judge.

Look at what Paul says in verse 1. "How are you going to judge someone when you are involved in the same thing." Why are so many pastors committing suicide, quitting, and walking away from the pulpit? One of the reasons is, that the struggle a lot of Pastors have to deal with is pastoring people who feel it's okay for them to fall short. Okay, for them to fall into temptation. Okay, for them to sin when they get weak. However, if the Pastor commits one 'uh oh', then he is judged, criticized and nailed to the cross. When the same ones that are accusing him are committing the same sins.

I remember, one time, I decided to go place flyers advertising our ministry on people's cars at a nightclub, since I heard that's where most church folks go before church. While I was placing flyers on the cars, one of the disciples that attends our ministry saw me putting flyers on the cars. She asked me, "Pastor, what are you doing here?" I replied, "Well, I was passing out flyers." The question was, "What are you doing here?" My purpose was to do ministry. The point I'm trying to make is this. She thought it was okay for her to go to the club, but thought it was strange for me to put flyers inviting people at the club to church. I can only imagine what she would have thought if I was in the club.

Paul says, as Believers, we should never put ourselves in the position of a judge. GOD already has that position covered. Look at what he says in verses 2-3. *We know that GOD's judgment is right when HE condemns people for doing these things. When you judge people for doing these things but then do them yourself, do you think you will escape GOD's judgment?*

Even if someone is dead wrong, let GOD be the one to judge them. You just stay in your lane and be a messenger. What are some of the dangers of becoming self-righteous? One of the dangers is, that not only will we start judging the unbelievers for their sins, but we will also start judging each other. We will start feeling that just because our sin is not their sin, then their sin is greater than our sins. We will start believing that our faith makes us more acceptable to GOD than them. That GOD is quicker to forgive us for our sins than HE is for theirs.

Verse 4 says *Do you have contempt for GOD, who is very kind to you, puts up with you, and deals patiently with you? Don't you realize that it is GOD's kindness that is trying to lead you to HIM and change the way you think and act?* If I'm too busy judging you for your sins, because I think your sins are greater than mine, I will start thinking that I am more presentable and acceptable to GOD, because of my faith than you are. That causes me not to get deliverance from my sins.

Even if my sins are not your sins, just the mere fact that I have sinned disqualifies me from sitting on the seat of judgment. Watch this, even in the midst of all my faith that GOD has accepted as righteousness still disqualifies me. In verse 4 GOD says "Even in the midst of your mess-ups, AM I not kind to you? Don't I still put up with you and deal with you patiently until you repent? Then who are you to criticize and judge someone else."

To those who try to do HIS job, GOD says, in verse 5 *Since you are stubborn and don't want to change the way you think and act, you are adding to the anger that GOD will have against you on that day when GOD vents HIS anger. At that time GOD will reveal that HIS decisions are fair.* GOD is saying, "I got this!" You just focus on yourself and accomplishing your assignment.

Verse 5 continues by saying *of the righteous judgment of GOD.* When GOD judges, HE judges right. HE doesn't judge according to someone else's opinion. When GOD judges, HE judges according to HIS Word. GOD's Word never changes, but man's opinion is forever changing. Anytime you want to start confusion, get out of your lane, and get into someone else's lane with your opinion. I can guarantee you, that you will get confusion every time.

Even if there's a situation whereby we can judge, we can't judge according to our self-righteousness. We need to judge like GOD. Judge righteously. We need to judge according to GOD's Word and not our own opinions. Do you know how many people in the Body of CHRIST are more concerned about man's opinions than they are about GOD's approval?

Would you rather have GOD judge you according to HIS Word, or have man judge you according to their opinions? If we would rather be judged by GOD only, then why is it so easy for us to judge others with our opinion? Remember what JESUS said in John 7:24. Do not judge according to appearance, your opinions, but judge with righteous judgment. Our righteous judgments should help restore other Believers to continue in well-doing. Our opinions only cause confusion.

Verse 6 lets us know the reason why GOD, the Ultimate Judge, doesn't need miniature judges. GOD will pay all people back for what they have done. Verses 7 and 8 say *He will give everlasting life to those who search for glory, honor, and immortality by persisting in doing what is good. But HE will bring anger and fury on those who, in selfish pride, refuse to believe the truth and who follow what is wrong.*

As a Believer, the only time I am ever allowed to judge is when I judge righteously. At no time should I ever judge according to my opinion or with my opinion. The only time we are allowed to judge is when another Believer is caught up in their sins. We only judge them righteously to restore them and not to shame them. When we make righteous judgments, it reminds them of what the Word of GOD says. At no time are we ever supposed to judge an unbeliever. We're supposed to witness the message of JESUS CHRIST to them. If I tell an unbeliever they're going to hell because of the sin they're practicing, that's in error.

The truth is, they're not going to hell because of the sins they are practicing. They are going to hell because they have not accepted salvation. A lot of people feel like they are not going to hell because they don't sin. A person not accepting the free gift of salvation, causes them to miss heaven.

What's sad is, that a lot of unbelievers will end up going to hell, because when they came in contact with a Believer, instead of the Believer offering them the message of the Gospel, they criticized and judged them for their sins. What brings conviction? GOD's Word. Wouldn't it be easier to witness The Gospel first? When they learn more of GOD's Word, it will convict them of their sins.

Verses 7 and 8 say that GOD will give everlasting life for those who seek to live righteous and punishment for those who choose to live wrong. As a matter of fact, verses 7 and 8 go with verses 9 through 11. *There will be suffering and distress for every person who does evil, for Jews first and Greeks as well. But there will be glory, honor, and peace for every person who does what is good, for Jews first and Greeks as well. GOD does not play favorites.*

What do verses 7 through 11 sound like? It sounds like what Paul was talking about in chapter 1. You will know those who GOD has approved, because they live by faith. Those who live by faith search for glory, honor, and immortality by persisting to do what is right. They choose to live by faith and persist in doing what's right, and are rewarded with everlasting life. Those whose lifestyles contradict GOD's truth, because they choose to live in unrighteousness, will be punished. Why? The answer is found in verse 11. *GOD does not play favorites.* This means everybody will have to deal with the consequences of how they chose to live.

Paul says, 'It doesn't matter what you call yourself, if you choose to live by GOD's truths, then you will reap good consequences. If you choose to disobey GOD's truths and live how you choose, then you will reap bad consequences." I think one of the problems in the Body of CHRIST is, that we get frustrated with people who claim to be Believers because they don't live by GOD's truths. And since they say they are Believers, we expect them to live by what they say they believe. When they don't, we get frustrated and disappointed. There's an old saying that says, "What doesn't come out in the wash will eventually come out in the rinse."

We shouldn't allow other people's failures to do what's right to frustrate us because those who live by faith, what does the text say? They are persistent in doing what's right, and persistent in seeking GOD's glory. Watch this, they are persistent in seeking GOD's approval. When you are seeking GOD's approval, you care less about man's opinions. What that says to me is, that you have more people claiming to be Believers than those who are actually Believers.

It shouldn't frustrate us that those that claim to be Believers don't live by what they say they believe. Paul said, "If you are truly a Believer, then you will live by what you say you believe". True Believers don't just talk the talk. They try to walk their talk. We walk by what we say we believe. We live by what we say we believe. Watch this, even if we fall short, verse 7 says we continue in well-doing.

Sin doesn't stop us from trying to live right. In verses 12 and 13, Paul says here's the reason. *Here's the reason: Whoever sins without having laws from GOD will still be condemned to destruction. And whoever has laws from GOD and sins will still be judged by them. People who merely listen to laws from GOD don't have GOD's approval. Rather, people who do what those laws demand will have GOD's approval.*

Wow! This is so deep. Here's why it's so dangerous to claim to be a Believer and not live by what you say you believe. The worst thing you can do is be a hearer, and then still refuse to be a doer. Watch very closely what Paul says in verse 13. People who only hear GOD's Word, but choose not to live by GOD's word, GOD rejects them. You can say you are a Believer all day long. But, if your lifestyle says differently, GOD rejects you. I wouldn't want to be rejected by GOD just because of my lifestyle.

In verse 12 Paul says Whoever sins without the law of GOD, which is the unbeliever, will perish. And those who sin with the law of GOD, those who have heard the law, verse 13 goes on to say, just because you have heard it does not justify you if you're not willing to do it. A true Believer's behavior resembles what they say they believe.

GOD only honors those who are willing to live by HIS Word. HE rewards those who choose to live by HIS Word. Once I become a hearer of the Word, I must make a decision. Do I seek after righteousness and be a doer of the Word, or do I choose to live wrong regardless of the word I've heard? I don't know about you, but I would rather be honored and rewarded for trying to live right than be rejected for living wrong.

GOD Will Judge People Who Are Not Jewish
Verses 14-29

After Paul breaks that down for us in verses 12 and 13, he gives us an example in verse 14. Not only does he give us an example, but in verses 14 through 16, Paul pretty much says that no one has an excuse. *For example, whenever non-Jews, those who don't have laws from GOD, do by nature the things that Moses' Teachings contain, they are a law to themselves. Even though they don't know any of the laws from GOD. They show that some requirements found in Moses' Teachings are written in their hearts without knowing the laws of GOD; their consciences speak to them. Their thoughts accuse them on one occasion and defend them on another. This happens as they face the day when GOD, through CHRIST JESUS, will judge people's secret thoughts. He will use the Good News that I am spreading to make that judgment.*

Even if you try to say that you didn't know, Paul said, your conscience should tell you what's right and what's wrong. No one will be able to stand before GOD and say, "I didn't know." The truth has been made available. What you decided to do with that truth determines your consequences. Matthew 24:14 (KJV) says, *And this Gospel of the kingdom will be preached in all the world as a witness to all the nations, and then the end will come.* Again, nobody will be able to say, "I didn't know." Watch what JESUS said in Matthew. The end will not come until everyone has at least heard the Gospel. Rather you accepted it or rejected it, at least you won't be able to say you didn't hear it.

After Paul deals with those who accept it and those who reject it, those who choose to believe and those who choose not to believe, then he deals with the hypocrites, those who say they believe, but choose not to practice what they believe. You have those who believe and practice what they believe. You have those who say they believe, but really don't believe, because their lifestyle shows us what they truly believe. Then you have a third group which I considered the most dangerous out of all of them, those that believe, but don't practice what they believe. They know The Word, but they don't follow The Word they know. They feel that just because they practice religion, they don't have to practice what they believe, because they feel like GOD is pleased.

There is a real big danger for those who believe, but do not practice what they believe. Look at what Paul says in verses 17-23. *You call yourself a Jew, rely on the laws in Moses' Teachings, brag about your GOD, know what HE wants, and distinguish right from wrong because you have been taught Moses' Teachings. You are confident that you are a guide for the blind, a light to those in the dark, an instructor of ignorant people, and a teacher of children because you have the full content of knowledge and truth in Moses' Teachings. As you teach others, are you failing to teach yourself? As you preach against stealing, are you stealing? As you tell others not to commit adultery, are you committing adultery? As you treat idols with disgust, are you robbing temples? As you brag about the laws in Moses' Teachings, are you dishonoring GOD by ignoring Moses' Teachings?*

Paul starts by saying in verse 17, "You call yourself a Believer and know The Law and even boast about GOD. You are quick to tell other people what The Word of GOD says. The problem is you don't practice it yourself." This is scary. Especially for those who are responsible for teaching GOD's Word. I could never understand how a pastor who knows what The Word of GOD says about sin, but still chooses to participate in it. Especially, when you know what GOD's Word says.

In verse 21 Paul questions them, "While you are teaching others, are you not teaching yourself?" In other words, how can you know the truth and not practice the truth? Look at what he says in verse 23. "You are dishonoring GOD by ignoring Moses' Teachings?" When you know the truth and choose not to practice the truth, not only are you dishonoring GOD, Paul says in verse 24 "GOD's name is cursed among the nations because of you."

Anyone who believes GOD's Word, but chooses not to practice it dishonors and curses GOD's name before nations. Paul uses the Jews to express his point. They were so caught up in Moses's Law, and the main ones not following The Law. By claiming to be GOD's people, they were bringing shame to GOD's name, because they refused to practice what they believed.

Wow! Did y'all catch that? When you call yourself a Christian, but refuse to live like a Christian, verse 23 says not only are we dishonoring GOD, but we also bring shame to HIS name. We embarrass GOD. If I'm going to be identified by my sins, it's better that I don't tell people that I am a Christian. If I choose not to live according to GOD's Word, it is better for me not to even say I'm a follower of CHRIST.

A true Believer does not follow a religion. They follow GOD, are disciple of CHRIST, and are not a follower of a religion. A person who believes but chooses not to practice what they believe feels that because of their loyalty to their religion/ministry, it makes them acceptable to GOD. If I feel that I am acceptable to GOD because of my loyalty to my religion, then that excuses me from practicing what I say I believe. I can teach about stealing, but it doesn't stop me from stealing. I can teach about lying, but it doesn't stop me from lying. I can teach about sin, but it doesn't stop me from practicing it. Why? I feel that I am acceptable to GOD, because of my loyalty to the ministry. Not realizing that not only am I dishonoring GOD, but I am also cursing HIS name.

In verses 25-29 Paul says, *Circumcision is valuable if you follow Moses' laws. If you don't follow those laws, your circumcision amounts to uncir-*

cumcision." So if a man does what Moses' Teachings demand, won't he be considered circumcised even if he is uncircumcised? The uncircumcised man who carries out what Moses' Teachings say will condemn you for not following them. He will condemn you in spite of the fact that you are circumcised and have Moses' Teachings in writing. A person is not a Jew because of his appearance, nor is circumcision a matter of how the body looks. Rather, a person is a Jew inwardly, and circumcision is something that happens in a person's heart. Circumcision is spiritual, not just a written rule. That person's praise will come from GOD, not from people.

What good is your ritual if you're going to disobey GOD? Paul says, just because you were circumcised, or just because you are baptized does not make you acceptable to GOD. You become acceptable to GOD by obeying HIM. GOD honors those who are obedient, not because they say they are a Believer. A true Believer is not someone who has changed what is on the outside, but is one who has changed what's on the inside. Sooner or later, what's on the inside will show up on the outside. What shows on the outside should never contradict what has been changed on the inside. Paul is saying, you can't be a Believer on the inside, but resemble a sinner on the outside.

Chapter 3

We All Fall Short

Everyone Is a Sinner
Verses 1-20

In chapter 3, Paul uses the Jews as his reference to speaking to the Christians Believers. Paul is dealing with the whole issue of being a Jew. So, to understand Paul's message and the method of his message, where Paul says "Jew", in your mind replace the word "Jew" with "Believer" to get a better understanding of Paul's message. The same concept that applied to the Jews, back then, also applies to the Believers today. Here are the comparisons. The Jews and Moses' Law and The Christian Believers and the Holy Bible.

For some reason, the Jews felt that just because they were considered as "GOD's People," that gave them the right to look down and judge other people. Paul was trying to make them understand, that just because they were willing to follow a ritual did not make them right. GOD only honors those who are willing to practice what they believe; you can be a hearer and not a doer.

Verse 1, *Is there any advantage, then, in being a Jew? Or is there any value in being circumcised?* Paul says, "If my title and my ritual do not bring me salvation, is there an advantage of being a Jew/Believer?" Now, remember what Paul said in chapter 2, "You're not a Believer because of what you choose to practice, you are a Believer because of how you choose to live."

Paul answers his own question in verse 2. *There are all kinds of advantages. First of all, GOD entrusted Believers with HIS Word.* Believers have a responsibility to live by HIS Word. If I'm walking around with the title of a Believer, because I say I am a Believer, but I choose not to live according to HIS Word, then I am not honoring GOD. I'm bringing shame to HIS name.

I want us to pay attention to verses 3 and 4. *What if some of them were unfaithful? Can their unfaithfulness cancel GOD's faithfulness? That would be unthinkable! GOD is honest, and everyone else is a liar, as Scripture says, "So you hand down justice when you speak, and you win your case in court.* Let's take a look at verse 3 again. *What if some of them*, them who? The Jews/Believers did not believe? *Can their unbelief cancel GOD's faithfulness?* Paul says in verse 4, "Certainly not!"

When people say, "I don't go to church anymore, because of the people," what they are saying is, "That's just my excuse for not going to church." Just because you had a run-in with a hypocrite, doesn't make GOD a liar. Watch this. Even if I misinterpret Scripture, that doesn't make GOD wrong. I'm wrong! By me being wrong shouldn't make you turn away from GOD or The Church. When people blame The Church for their absence, my thought is, that you just didn't want to be at church anyway. Now, you just have an excuse.

Paul says, just because someone calls themselves a Believer, but walks in disbelief does not change the character or the nature of GOD. GOD is still GOD whether I choose to practice what I believe or not. If GOD doesn't change, then my faith shouldn't change just because people decided to change. Paul says that makes absolutely no sense. You can't blame GOD because someone else chose to act foolishly.

Here's why Paul says you bring shame to GOD's name when you choose not to live according to HIS Word. It makes GOD look unfair.

Verses 5 and 6, *But if what we do wrong shows that GOD is fair, what should we say? Is GOD unfair when HE vents HIS anger on us? (I'm arguing the way humans would.) That's unthinkable! Otherwise, how would GOD be able to judge the world?* In other words, you can't call yourself a

Believer, live a lifestyle of sin, and GOD allows you to go to heaven. But, then someone who is an unbeliever lives the same lifestyle, and GOD sends them to hell.

If we live a sinful lifestyle, it brings dishonor to GOD and brings shame to HIS name. We make GOD look like a hypocrite. The unbeliever will think, "How are you going to heaven, and I'm going to hell when we both are practicing the same lifestyle just because you are a so-called 'Believer'? That's not fair. Well, let me become a Believer so I can still practice my sin and go to heaven." So, Paul says in verse 6 that's *unthinkable*/crazy!

Verse 7, *If my lie increases the glory that GOD receives by showing that GOD is truthful, why am I still judged as a sinner?* You don't go to heaven just because you call yourself a Believer. You go to heaven because you chose to live right. When you feel like you're entitled to go to heaven just because you are a Jew/Believer, Paul explains this type of attitude in verse 8. *Or can we say, "Let's do evil so that good will come from it"? Some slander us and claim that this is what we say. They are condemned, and that's what they deserve.* If I go to heaven just because I hold the title of being a Believer, then what does it matter if I choose to sin or live right? I'm going to heaven anyway.

Paul says that's the problem with Jews and Believers. They feel like just because they hold the title of a Believer their title is their ticket into heaven. Some people feel that just because they were born a Jew and even if they didn't believe, by them being Jewish gives them the right to GOD's Kingdom. Just like you have some Christians that believe just because they call themselves Christians, they automatically go to heaven.

Paul says that's the furthest thing from the truth. When we think our title of being a Believer gives us access to heaven, it causes us not to be accountable for how we live here on earth. GOD is only going to accept those who chose to believe and chose to live right. Everybody else HE's going to reject. Regardless of their title.

- Regardless of how big their Bible was.
- Regardless of how much time they spent in church.
- Regardless of how long their dress was.
- Regardless of them singing in the choir.
- Regardless of them preaching in the pulpit.

If you choose to believe and choose to live righteously, GOD is going to accept you. Not only is GOD going to accept you, but Paul said, "GOD is going to honor and reward you". If you chose to believe or not, and chose to live unrighteous, GOD is going to reject you. The worst thing a person can do is choose to believe and bust hell wide open, because they chose to live unrighteous. Just because you hold the title of a Believer doesn't give you keys to the Kingdom. Nor, does it give you access to go to heaven. I wonder how many people who call themselves Believers think they're on their way to heaven, but their lifestyle and their disobedience are sending them to hell?

Paul told the Jews/Believers, you call yourself a Believer and know The Law and even boast about GOD. You are quick to tell other people what the Word of GOD says, but the problem is, you don't practice it yourself. How can you know the truth and not practice the truth? Paul said you dishonor GOD when you know the truth, but ignore it.

Can you imagine all the Believers that know the truth, but choose not to live by it? My question is, how do you go to hell from the pew? By being a Believer and refusing to live by what you say you believe. If I say I am a Believer, a follower of CHRIST, I am responsible to live according to GOD's Word. If I don't, I bring shame to GOD's name. No matter how much talent I have. No matter how many followers who choose to follow me. If I know the truth, but refuse to live by the truth, I dishonor GOD.

Verses 9 and 10 *What then? Are we better than they? Not at all. For we have previously charged both Jews and Greeks that they are all under sin, as Scripture says, "Not one person has GOD's approval."*

Wow! Did y'all catch that? Paul said, "There is not one person that does not need GOD's approval." I don't care who they are. You cannot be a Jew and live foul. Just like you can't be a Christian and live foul either. The only people that GOD accepts into HIS Kingdom are those who choose to believe and those who strive to live right. Even if you happen to fall short, GOD accepts those who continue in well doing.

Let's understand the dynamics of what Paul is saying. The Jews thought they belonged to GOD, because of their race and not by their faith. In verse 9 they said because of our race, aren't we better than them? Don't our race set us apart? Doesn't our race make us acceptable to GOD? Paul said, of course not! We all were born under sin. No one was born into righteousness.

So, because of their race, they thought they automatically belonged to GOD. They thought because their title of being a Jew made them acceptable to GOD. They thought just because they call themselves Christians that made them acceptable to GOD. Paul tells them in verse 10 that your title as a Christian/Jew doesn't make you righteous. How you choose to live, makes you righteous.

For some reason or another, we think just because someone holds the title of being a Christian automatically makes them one. And, just because they are in church, means they are saved. Just because I decide to stand in the garage doesn't make me a car. Just because someone goes to Church doesn't make them a Christian. Just because someone has a religion doesn't mean they have a relationship.

GOD doesn't approve what we choose to practice, HE accepts us based on what we choose to believe. Paul said, "I don't care what your title is, not one person has GOD's approval. There is none righteous, no, not one! Your race doesn't make you righteous." Your title as a Christian doesn't make you righteous. How you choose to live makes you righteous.

Verses 11 and 12 *There is none that understandeth, there is none that seeketh after GOD. They are all gone out of the way, they are together become unprofitable; there is none that doeth good, no, not one.* But hold up, I am a Jew! I'm a Christian. What do you mean there is none?

Paul is not trying to discredit their title as a Believer, but the problem was and the problem now is, their title caused them to neglect the way they were supposed to live. For some reason, we think just because someone holds the title of being a Christian automatically makes them one.

Look at what Paul says when you just hold the title of a Believer in verses 13 – 18. *Their throat is an open sepulcher; with their tongues they have used deceit; the poison of asps is under their lips: Whose mouth is full of cursing and bitterness: Their feet are swift to shed blood: Destruction and misery are in their ways: And the way of peace have they not known: There is no fear of GOD before their eyes.*

Could you imagine holding a title as a Believer, but, yet having no fear of GOD? Paul says in verse 18 *they have no fear of GOD before their eyes.* In other words, they are in your face with their sin. They are out in the open with their sin. They are identified by their sin. The reason there is no shame to them about their sin is, that they have no fear of GOD. So, verses 13 through 18 speak about those who have a religion, but don't have a relationship.

The reason they don't have a relationship with GOD is, that they don't fear GOD. When you fear GOD, there are just some things you won't do. Even if by chance you mess around and do them, because you fear GOD, it brings shame to you when you stand before GOD.

Question. Have you ever done something and you knew you had to get it right before GOD? And, when you decided to take it before GOD, you could feel your spirit man going before GOD with his head hung down in shame? That's because you fear GOD.

Paul said, those who don't fear GOD, try to take their mess before GOD, and they don't feel any shame. They try to stand before GOD looking a hot mess.

- They stand in the pulpit, looking like a hot mess.
- They lead praise and worship, looking like a hot mess.
- They sing in the choir, looking like a hot mess.
- They participate in the service, looking like a hot mess.

While looking a hot mess before GOD, they have no shame. Why is this? Verse 18 says *they have no fear of GOD before their eyes.* If they don't care how they look before GOD, they really don't care how they look before men. It's no problem for them to bring their mess before a holy GOD, because they have no fear. And, since they have no fear, they have no shame. So, they'll come before a holy GOD with their sin on and feel no shame. Why? They have no fear.

Verses 19 and 20, *Now we know that whatever the law says, it says to those who are under the law, that every mouth may be stopped, and all the world may become guilty before GOD. Therefore by the deeds of the law no flesh will be justified in HIS sight, for by the law is the knowledge of sin.* In other words, as a true Believer, you don't have a choice, but to live right. Paul says, to say that you are a Believer means, you are accountable to live by what you say you believe. In verse 20 he says, *by the deeds of the law no flesh will be justified.*

The purpose of The Law is not to justify. It's so we can identify our sins. The moment you can identify your sins, it makes you realize that you need to be saved. When I don't identify my sins, then I try to justify my sins. That's why it's so important for us to live right. Even if it doesn't bring any shame to you, Paul said it brings shame to GOD. GOD is not going to allow anyone to continue to shame HIS name.

GOD Gives Us His Approval as a Gift
Verses 21-31

In verses 21 and 22, Paul is about to back up everything he's been telling us since chapter 1. *But now the righteousness of GOD apart from the law is revealed, being witnessed by the Law and the Prophets, even the righteousness of GOD, through faith in JESUS CHRIST, to all and on all who believe. For there is no difference;* Once again, to all who believe by faith, GOD takes their faith and counts it as righteousness. Therefore, making them acceptable before GOD. There is no way GOD can make me acceptable, and I choose to still live in sin.

Verse 23 is what a lot of Believers don't want to admit. *For all have sinned and fall short of the glory of GOD.* Stop! True Believers when they sin and have fallen short, they continue in well doing. Those who sin and fall short and keep sinning, are the ones that try to justify their sin so they can keep sinning. They don't continue in well doing. They continue in their sin.

Verse 24, *They receive GOD's approval freely by an act of HIS kindness through the price CHRIST JESUS paid to set us free from sin.* Wow! Did y'all catch that? Look at what verse 24 says. *We have been justified freely by HIS grace through the redemption in JESUS CHRIST.* If I have been freed from sin, then how could it be easy for me to freely live in sin? It's not possible. Yes, it's possible to mess up. Yes, it's possible to fall short. But, when you have been truly set free and you have been truly delivered, Paul said, "It's not possible to hold GOD's truth and walk in unrighteousness."

Verses 25 and 26 *GOD showed that CHRIST is the throne of mercy where GOD's approval is given through faith in CHRIST's blood. In HIS patience GOD waited to deal with sins committed in the past. HE waited so that HE could display HIS approval at the present time. This shows that HE is a GOD of justice, a GOD who approves of people who believe in JESUS.* I can't be born into it. I have to live by faith. How I live demonstrates what I choose to believe. I can't say I believe it if I'm not willing to live by it.

Watch this. I can only brag about being a Believer when I choose to live by what I believe. Paul says in verses 27 and 28, *So, do we have anything to brag about? Bragging has been eliminated. On what basis was it eliminated? On the basis of our own efforts? No, indeed! Rather, it is eliminated on the basis of faith. We conclude that a person has GOD's approval by faith, not by his own efforts.* In other words, I can't brag about being a Believer unless I choose to live by what I say I believe. When I live by what I say I believe, I don't boast in myself, but I boast in the GOD that saved me.

- I boast in the GOD that changed me.
- I boast in the GOD that delivered me.
- I boast in the GOD that has set me free.

Now, if nothing has blessed your spirit up to this point, verses 29 through 31 are a blessing all in itself. Paul asks a question, *Is GOD only the GOD of the Jews? Isn't HE also the GOD of people who are not Jewish? Certainly, HE is, since it is the same GOD who approves circumcised people by faith and uncircumcised people through this same faith. Are we abolishing Moses' Teachings by this faith? That's unthinkable! Rather, we are supporting Moses' Teachings.*

Paul says GOD never accepted the Jews by their rituals. GOD has always accepted Believers by their faith. Whether they were circumcised or not, GOD accepts us by faith. Whether they are white or black, GOD accepts us according to our faith. There's only one GOD. Since HE created all, then all can be saved. All can be changed. All can be delivered. All can be set free. All are justified the same way; by faith.

Watch how clever Paul was. In verse 31 Paul says, "So, then, does our faith destroy Moses' teachings? He says of course not!" We should never take The Law to establish our faith. Our faith should always determine what we choose to follow. Before there was a law, GOD accepted Abraham by faith. The Law was created to remind us what is acceptable to GOD according to our faith. It was never supposed to control us by replacing what we believe by faith.

Chapter 4

We Have GOD's Approval by Faith

In chapter 4, Paul deals with us having GOD's approval by faith. Especially, those that choose to live by faith. Grace sees that we are serious about what we believe, and we truly believe and want to be saved. Grace saves us, and GOD takes our faith and makes us acceptable before HIM. Grace takes our faith and examines it to see if it's real or not. To see if there are any hidden motives; "Oh, you just want to come in to stir up mess? Denied!"

This now takes us into chapter 4. Now, before diving into chapter 4, let me ask a question. How important is it for you to have GOD's approval? Remember, what we've already talked about. When you are seeking GOD's approval, you care less about man's opinion. When you are really serious about what GOD thinks, it dictates how you choose to live. It even dictates the words you choose to say. The flipside to that is, that if I don't care how I choose to live or what comes out of my mouth, I'm not all that serious about what GOD thinks.

Verses 1 – 3 *What can we say that we have discovered about our ancestor Abraham? If Abraham had GOD's approval because of something he did, he would have had a reason to brag. But, he could not brag to GOD about it. What does Scripture say? "Abraham believed GOD, and that faith was regarded by GOD to be HIS approval of Abraham."*

Remember, the whole message Paul dealt with in chapter 3. The Believers thought just because they held the title of being Believers or Jews, it made them acceptable to GOD. Paul tells them in verses 1 – 3, "If you all really want to get technical, let's consider Abraham where it all started from. Abraham was acceptable to GOD based on his faith and what he chose to believe, not what he did. Abraham was counted righteous not because of what he chose to practice."

So, practicing religion doesn't make you acceptable to GOD. Having faith in GOD makes you acceptable to HIM. Abraham was accepted because of his faith, not because he sang in the choir or sat in the pulpit and wore a collar.

Watch this, Abraham's faith preceded his obedience. In other words, because of his faith, it caused him to be obedient. He believed GOD therefore, he obeyed GOD. Verses 4 and 5, *When people work, their pay is not regarded as a gift but something they have earned. However, when people don't work but believe GOD, the one who approves ungodly people, their faith is regarded as GOD's approval.*

Did y'all catch that? You can't work your way into GOD's approval. You have to believe your way into HIS approval. When I feel like I'm acceptable to GOD because of my practices, that puts GOD in debt. As if GOD owes me something. As if GOD owes me HIS approval. Because, then I feel like the more I work, the more GOD owes me.

GOD cannot be put in debt by anyone. Singing in the choir doesn't save me. Sitting in the pulpit doesn't save me. Working in the church doesn't save me or make me acceptable to GOD. I can work in The Church and still be on my way to hell. When someone thinks their work makes them acceptable, they exhaust themselves working in The Church, but then turn around and live any kind of way they choose outside the church. Look at who GOD approves. Verse 4, *ungodly people* who believe in HIM by faith. So, once again, all have sinned. Since all have sinned, then all need to have faith to be saved.

Verses 6 –8 *David says the same thing about those who are blessed: GOD approves of people without their earning it. David said, "Blessed are those whose disobedience is forgiven and whose sins are pardoned. Blessed is the person whom the LORD no longer considers sinful."* David said, blessed are those who used to live a life of sin and are now acceptable by GOD. Why would I allow anyone to make me feel bad about my past life? David said, "Blessed is the person who GOD doesn't no longer consider a sinner." For some reason, we are ashamed of our past life, because of what other people may say or think. Those we are worried about have to be saved themselves.

In chapter 3 Paul said *we all have sinned.* This means all of us who have been saved by grace are ex-sinners. Noticed he called us sinners and not by our individual sin. If GOD doesn't judge our past sins, who are we to judge someone's sins GOD saved them from? If GOD doesn't make me feel bad for my past mistakes when I was a sinner, why should I allow someone to make me feel bad now that I'm saved? Regardless of the sin I was in.

David said blessed are those who used to live a life of sin. Notice he said used to. David didn't say, blessed are those who sin. I don't want you to think, that the more you sin, the blessed you are. As if, you need to add up some more sins to your account. David is saying, don't feel bad about your past sins. If our sins were going to send us to hell, you can shout because now you are acceptable to GOD. Your sins made you rejected by GOD. Your faith has made you acceptable to GOD. Should I pause here for a shout?

Here's why David says we are blessed. Not because of our sins, but because our faith has made us the righteousness of GOD. You are blessed because your sins have been forgiven and covered.

Verses 9 – 11 are very important. *Are only the circumcised people blessed, or are uncircumcised people blessed as well? We say, "Abraham's faith was regarded as GOD's approval of him." How was his faith regarded as GOD's approval? Was he circumcised or was he uncircumcised at that time? He had not been circumcised. Abraham's faith was regarded as GOD's approval while he was still uncircumcised.* In other words, Abraham was accepted by GOD before he was circumcised. The mark of circumcision is the seal of that approval. He received circumcision, not for GOD's approval, but to show that he had already been approved.

Verse 12, *Therefore, he is the father of every Believer who is not circumcised, and their faith, too, is regarded as GOD's approval of them. He is also the father of those who not only are circumcised but also are following in the footsteps of his faith. Our father Abraham had that faith before he was circumcised.* It wasn't anything Abraham did to receive GOD's approval. It was only by his faith.

The Jews thought the only way to be acceptable to GOD was by circumcision. Paul said Abraham became acceptable before circumcision. Those who think baptism brings salvation, according to Paul, we became acceptable to GOD before baptism. You receive salvation at the point of belief; not at the point of works or baptism/circumcision. Paul made it plain and simple, we baptize out of obedience, not to bring salvation. My lifestyle should demonstrate what I believe.

Look at what he says in verse 12. *We are connected to Abraham because we follow in the footsteps of his faith*, not by his works. That's good! I do what I do out of obedience, because I truly believe GOD for real. A person who truly believes and trust GOD for real is willing to obey GOD for real. The Jews felt like they were acceptable to GOD, because they kept the Mosaic Laws and the rituals they were practicing. It had nothing to do with believing in GOD or living right. They felt if they practiced their tradition, then GOD accepted them and was pleased with them.

Look at verse 13. *So it was not by obeying Moses' Teachings that Abraham or his descendants received the promise that he would inherit the world. Rather, it was through GOD's approval of his faith.* In other words, y'all want to make your practices of the Mosaic Law, Bible. Abraham had not even received the Mosaic Laws and GOD accepted him. As a matter of fact, the Mosaic Laws were not even established. Abraham was accepted by GOD before the ritual. How are you going to take the ritual and now make it a requirement? In other words, how are your laws going to determine if GOD is pleased when GOD accepted Abraham before Moses' Laws were even created? It wasn't by what Abraham was practicing that made him acceptable to GOD. It was because of what Abraham believed. Genesis 15:6, *Then Abram believed the LORD, and the LORD regarded that faith to be HIS approval of Abram.*

Verse 14, *If those who obey Moses' Teachings are the heirs, then faith is useless and the promise is worthless.* Paul said, "If it was all about Moses' teachings, then what good is having faith. Without faith, the promises of GOD are worthless." Watch how profound this is. Remember how strict the Jews were regarding the law? Paul says, "GOD does not give us HIS promises through The Law, but HE gives us HIS promises through the righteousness of our faith."

When we feel like our work causes GOD to approve us, then we put GOD in debt to us. Do you know that there are people who actually believe that if they come to church, then GOD owes them a blessing? So, they come to church, work, then expect GOD to reward them because they came. They believe if they bring their tithes, GOD owes them a blessing.

I don't bring my tithes because I'm looking for blessings. I bring my tithes out of obedience. Malachi 3:15 GOD says, *Bring all the tithe into the storehouse so that there may be food in MY house. Test ME in this way,"* says the LORD of Armies. *"See if I won't open the windows of heaven for you and flood you with blessings.* Because of my obedience, GOD then rewards it.

When my work is not done out of obedience, then my work is done out of expectancy. In other words, I'm only doing this so GOD can bless me with that. When I work expecting something, I'm telling GOD, "You owe me, because I did this." GOD meets us on our level of faith, not on our level of work.

Verses 15 – 16, *The laws in Moses' Teachings bring about anger. But where laws don't exist, they can't be broken. Therefore, the promise is based on faith so that it can be a gift. Consequently, the promise is guaranteed for every descendant, not only for those who are descendants by obeying Moses' Teachings but also for those who are descendants by believing as Abraham did. He is the father of all of us,*

Our promises are based on what we believe and having faith in GOD, not because we work like crazy to be blessed by GOD. Look at what Paul says in verse 16. When we receive our promises based on our faith, then our promises become a gift from GOD. If we receive GOD's promises because of what we have done (work), then it becomes compensation. GOD wants our promises to be a gift and not a reimbursement.

I don't know about you, but I like that agreement better. All I have to do is have faith in GOD and trust in HIM with all my heart and not trust my own understanding, and HE gives me HIS promises. Instead of working expecting GOD to owe me something. Paul said, "Y'all are working too hard trying to follow every one of Moses' Laws. Why work for HIS promises when you can just have faith and receive HIS promises?" I'd rather have faith and receive GOD's promises than work for HIS promises. What about you?

If I preached, expecting a check, then that is going to be my reward. My blessings stop at that check. But, if I just preach out of obedience and because of my love for GOD, HE turns around and blessed me with HIS promises. If I just happen to receive a check, that's just an addition to HIS promises.

A lot of people shortchange themselves, because of what they are expecting in return. "LORD, I did this. Now I'm expecting for YOU to reimburse me for the work I've done." When I see people who are not consistent in their working or consistent in their service, that immediately tells me that they are working for compensation. Not because of their obedience or love for GOD. When I don't get my proper compensation, then I stop working. I stop showing up. I stop being committed. I stop being faithful. The only time I show up and work is when I want to be compensated for my labor.

- So, let me come to church, so I can be compensated.
- Let me sing in the choir, so I can be compensated.

- Let me preach the gospel, so I can be compensated.
- Let me pass out programs, so I can be compensated. Not because I love GOD and want to see the Kingdom grow, but because of what I'm expecting in return.

Being a disciple in the Kingdom is not like being an employee on your job. You don't work for compensation, you labor out of obedience and because of your love for GOD. You labor because you are a Kingdom citizen and not a company employee. We labor out of obedience, not because we're expecting HIS promises. I can't work for HIS promises. I have to trust GOD by faith for that. Any promise from GOD, such as healing, miracles, deliverances and breakthroughs I don't have to work for. It is given to me through the righteousness of my faith. If I need healing, I don't have to work for my healing. My healing will come through the righteousness of my faith.

Now before we read the next verses, I have a question for you. Who was the source of Abraham's faith? GOD. GOD alone, right? GOD promises don't come because I practiced a ritual; like jumping up three times and spinning around two. In the next verses, Paul says, our promises come through a source. So, we believe in the promises, because we trust the source.

Watch this. Don't miss this. I don't even trust in the promises. I only stand on the promises, because of who the Source is. My faith is in the Source which is GOD and HIM alone. It's easy for me to have faith, because I trust in the Source. When I put my faith in the promises and not the Source, I work because I want the promises and not necessarily the Source. It's the Source that supplies the promises.

A lot of people put their trust in GOD's promises. So, they trust the promises more than they trust the Source. When your dependency is on the promise and not the Source, then you feel unfulfilled when you get the promise, because you thought your happiness was going to be in the promise. GOD's promises don't have everything we need, GOD the Source does. Philippians 4:19 says, *And my GOD shall supply all your need according to HIS riches in glory by CHRIST JESUS.* I have faith in the Source, not the promise. I only believe the promise because of the Source.

In verses 17 – 22, Look at what the Source promises, *as Scripture says: "I have made you a father of many nations." Abraham believed when he stood in the presence of the GOD who gives life to dead people and calls into existence things that don't even exist. When there was nothing left to hope for, Abraham still hoped and believed. As a result, he became a father of many nations, as he had been told: "That is how many descendants you will have." Abraham didn't weaken. Through faith he regarded the facts: His body was already as good as dead now that he was about a hundred years old, and Sarah was unable to have children. He didn't doubt GOD's promise out of a lack of faith. Instead, giving honor to GOD for the promise, he became strong because of faith and was absolutely confident that GOD would do what HE promised. That is why his faith was regarded as GOD's approval of him.*

Look at verse 20 again. He didn't doubt GOD's promise out of a lack of faith. Instead, giving honor to GOD for the promise, he became strong because of faith. When your faith in GOD is about HIM and not HIS promises, that's when GOD knows HE can trust you with HIS promises. Can GOD trust you with HIS promises? Or, do you abandon GOD once you have received HIS promises until you are in need of another promise?

Look at verse 22. That is why his faith was regarded as GOD's approval of him. In other words, GOD says, when I know that you are with ME, because you want ME and not MY promises, then I know I can trust you with MY promises. Some people try to get with GOD because of what they can get from HIM. So, they show up when they want something from GOD. Their faith is not in GOD. Their faith is in HIS promises.

They master doing church, because they think that will bring them HIS promises. They follow rituals, because they feel that will bring them HIS promises. That's why the Bible tells us to *seek ye first the Kingdom of GOD and HIS righteousness, then all of these things shall be added.* (Matthew 6:33) I can't get the promises of GOD by seeking the things of GOD. I only get the promises of GOD by seeking GOD and living right.

Once again, it's only through the righteousness of our faith that we are able to receive HIS promises. Like Paul told us before, "When your faith in GOD is about GOD and not about HIS promises, that's when GOD knows HE can trust you with HIS promises." I want GOD just because HE's GOD, not because of HIS promises. Even if I don't receive another promise, I just want GOD.

Look at how Paul closes out chapter 4. Verses 23 – 25, *But the words "his faith was regarded as GOD's approval of him" were written not only for him but also for us. Our faith will be regarded as GOD's approval of us who believe in the one who brought JESUS, our Lord, back to life. JESUS, our Lord, was handed over to death because of our failures and was brought back to life so that we could receive GOD's approval.*

In order to be accepted by GOD, not only do I need to have the same type of faith as Abraham in the Old Testament had, but I need to know that through JESUS' death it paid the cost for my sins. With that belief and JESUS' sacrifice, I am made acceptable to GOD. We are acceptable to GOD by our faith, not by HIS promises.

If we are only acceptable to GOD through our faith, then why would anyone put all of their faith in GOD's promises? I trust the Source, not the promises. Once again, I only believe the promises, because of the Source. If you know you have a promise because of the Source, I'll give you a moment to shout before we go into chapter 5.

Chapter 5
At Peace With GOD

We Are at Peace With GOD, Because of JESUS
Verses 1-11

Chapter 4 taught us that faith determines if we are accepted or rejected by GOD. Some people think the more they do makes them more acceptable to GOD. It wasn't what Abraham was practicing that made him acceptable to GOD. It was what Abraham chose to believe. GOD does not give us HIS promises through The Law, but HE gives us HIS promises through the righteousness of our faith. GOD does not reward us according to our works. HE rewards us according to our faith. HE's going to open doors according to our faith. GOD meets us on our level of faith, not on our level of work.

When I receive GOD's promises based on my faith, HIS promises become a gift. If I receive GOD's promises because of what I have done, then it becomes compensation. GOD wants our promises to be a gift and not a reimbursement.

This now takes us into chapter 5. The theme of chapter 5 is found in verse 1. Look how Paul so eloquently carries us into chapter 5. *Now that we have GOD's approval by faith, we have peace with GOD because of what our Lord JESUS CHRIST has done.* Not only am I accepted by GOD because of my faith, but look at what Paul says in verse 1; we also have peace with GOD because of what JESUS has done. How can I be accepted by GOD according to my faith and know GOD is pleased with me because of my faith and not have peace?

If I choose to live by faith, and because of that faith I choose to live by makes me acceptable to GOD, there's no way I shouldn't have peace.

Regardless of the chaos, look at what Paul says in verse 1, "Because we have GOD's approval, because of the work JESUS has done, we have peace with GOD."

If I'm walking around timid, scared, and paranoid, it's because I don't have peace with GOD. If I'm not at peace, it's because I'm not living by faith. When I live according to my faith and my faith causes GOD to accept me, I then have peace with GOD.

Verse 2 says *Through CHRIST we can approach GOD and stand in HIS favor. So we brag because of our confidence that we will receive glory from GOD.* In the midst of the chaos and the confusion, not only will I have peace, but I have also been given access to stand in GOD's favor. All of this is going to take place, because of my faith and not my work. Paul says, "I can brag about my faith, not about my works."

The problem in the Body of CHRIST is, that people brag about their works, but they can't say anything about their faith. People who are not walking by faith do not have peace with GOD and access to stand in GOD's favor. You can always tell who they are because they are quick to brag about their works. They don't have anything to show that they have done with their faith.

Look at what Paul says in verse 2, We can stand and rejoice in hope. How can you stand and rejoice about your faith if you don't have any results of what your faith has done? With that being said, now I am under the persuasion that when people don't have anything to say about their faith, they have to rejoice in their works. Why? They don't have any evidence of what their faith has done. They don't have a choice but to talk about their works. They don't have any evidence of their faith. No faith equals no peace. No peace equals no results.

If I'm not at peace, it's because I'm not living by faith. If I am experiencing a trial or going through a storm and living by faith, the promise is, that I should have peace. You know when you have peace is when you can do what verse 2 says. Stand and rejoice in hope in your storm. The reason I'm able to rejoice in hope in my storm is that I understand that my storm is increasing my faith to trust in GOD. GOD will always meet us on our level of faith.

When you know your storm has a purpose, instead of being ashamed of it, you learn how to glorify in it. Not glorify because you came out of it, but because of the peace with GOD and the purpose of the storm you can glorify in the storm. According to verse 2, not only do we have peace with GOD when we live by faith, but Paul also said we have access to stand in GOD's favor. It's one thing to be able to stand before GOD. It's another thing to be able to stand before GOD with favor.

When Paul says we have access to stand before GOD *in HIS favor*, what does that mean to you? Whatever it is, it is a privilege. Meaning, that we're not qualified to even stand before GOD. But, because of JESUS, not only do we have access to stand in GOD's presence, but we have favor when we stand.

Because of JESUS' covering, when I stand before GOD, when GOD sees me, it's as if HE's looking at HIS Son JESUS. Paul gives us more understanding about all this in verses 3 and 4. *But that's not all. We also brag when we are suffering. We know that suffering creates endurance, endurance creates character, and character creates confidence.*

Verse 3 is very important. It tells us that even while suffering, we have peace in the suffering. The suffering is going to produce endurance, character, and even more hope. The trials that we have to endure are going to produce even more hope to trust GOD for even greater things. In the midst of the trial and me trusting in GOD, during the chaos, it's building my patience, character, and hope to trust GOD for even greater.

Everything I go through, causes me to trust GOD for something even greater, which also increases my faith. When you become accepted by GOD, problems and trials have a purpose. If I am going to go through something,

I'd rather it have a purpose. Do you know how many people go through unnecessary problems that have no purpose? As long as I am walking by faith, nothing I go through is unnecessary. Even if it seems unnecessary, it is still building my patience, character, and hope which causes me to trust GOD even greater.

Why don't I have to worry about whatever I may go through when I'm walking by faith? Because, I have the peace of GOD as it says in verse 1. While everyone else is worrying about what's going on around them, I'm trusting GOD, because I have peace. Verse 5 says, *We're not ashamed to have this confidence, because GOD's love has been poured into our hearts by the HOLY SPIRIT, who has been given to us.*

Paul says in verse 5 and this hope makes us not ashamed. For some reason or another, whenever we are going through something, we allow what we are going through to make us feel shameful or embarrassed. When we see someone going through something, we automatically think it's because they did something wrong. Or we are ashamed to expose what we're going through, because we are afraid it makes us look like we're not walking by faith. So, we camouflage what we're going through.

Paul says in verse 3 that when you know your trials have a purpose, instead of being ashamed of it, you glorify in it. You know and understand that the trial you're going through is building your patience, character, and even more hope. While everyone else is looking at you going through your trial, wondering if you're going to come out of it, you're looking at your trial as something that's making you better and not bitter.

The reason we're going to come out better and not bitter is that, in verse 5, Paul tells us how we're going to come out better. He says the love of GOD *has been poured into our hearts by the HOLY SPIRIT.* When the HOLY SPIRIT has been poured into your heart, you'll always come out better. Why should I feel ashamed about anything I have gone through when it has made me better? You're only bitter when it has not made you better.

Why should I be bitter about something that's making me better? Why should I feel ashamed about anything I go through when the HOLY SPIRIT has given me GOD's peace? The HOLY SPIRIT has given me GOD's love that's building patience, character, and more hope inside of me, increasing my faith and will cause me to trust GOD even greater. How many of you can tell GOD thank you for something you have gone through because it made you better?

The only one that can't understand what GOD is doing, is someone who is not walking by faith. Why should I allow someone who is not walking by faith to make me feel bad about something that's making me better? That's why it's so important who you are in covenant with. If they are not walking by faith, they will look at your trials as something that's against you instead of rejoicing with you because it's making you better.

After Paul tells us in verse 5 *that GOD's love has been poured into our hearts by the HOLY SPIRIT*, look at what he says in verses 6-8. Now, if this doesn't give you a reason to glory in your tribulation, I don't know what will. *Look at it this way: At the right time, while we were still helpless, CHRIST died for ungodly people. Finding someone who would die for a godly person is rare. Maybe someone would have the courage to die for a good person. CHRIST died for us while we were still sinners. This demonstrates GOD's love for us.*

Wow! Look at what Paul says. He said, "CHRIST died for us while we were yet sinners." Not died for those who are perfect, but those who were yet sinners. For all those who have never sinned or fallen short, He didn't die for you. He only died for the sinner. Paul said it's easy to be willing to die for someone who has never done any wrong. But, who in their right mind would give their life for somebody that's dead wrong? Who would sacrifice their life for someone that is guilty and deserves to die? CHRIST!

I don't think y'all see how profound this is. Paul said CHRIST died for us while we were still sinners. In other words, while we were in our sins, HE died for us. Not after we decided to stop sinning, but while we were sinning, HE died. HE was on HIS way to the cross while we were sinning to cover our sins so GOD could see us and not our sins.

When we stand before GOD, our faith takes JESUS's blood and covers our sins. Instead of GOD seeing our sins, HE sees the righteousness of JESUS' blood. Our blood is tainted, JESUS' blood is perfect. When HE takes HIS perfect blood and covers our tainted blood, instead of us looking like the sin we were in, we now look like the righteousness of GOD. That's why I don't have to be ashamed about my past sins. Everything that happened in my past HIS blood covers it.

Verses 9 and 10, *Since CHRIST's blood has now given us GOD's approval, we are even more certain that CHRIST will save us from GOD's anger. If the death of HIS Son restored our relationship with GOD while we were still HIS enemies, we are even more certain that, because of this restored relationship, the life of HIS Son will save us.*

I remember hearing a pastor permitting people to sin. He said, "We are still sinners, and sinners sin." Well, at least he got that part right because sinners do sin. But, when you have been accepted by GOD and HE has covered you in JESUS' blood, you are no longer considered a sinner. You no longer have an excuse to sin, even though you may sin. When CHRIST died, He didn't die for us to continue in sin. He died because of the sin we were in. Verse 10 says the death of JESUS restored our relationship with GOD. GOD does not have relationships with sinners.

If my faith in JESUS causes me to be the righteousness of GOD, how can I stand before GOD, covered in HIS righteousness and still identify myself as a sinner? Especially, when GOD considers me as righteous.

Those who GOD considers as the righteousness of HIMSELF, even though they fall short, Paul said they continue in *well-doing*. Only those who continue in their sins and live a lifestyle of sin are still considered sinners. Why? They are not covered in the righteousness of GOD. When

GOD sees them, HE sees their sins. When we stand before GOD, because of JESUS' blood, HE doesn't see a sinner, but HE sees HIS children. Why would I consider myself a sinner when GOD sees me as HIS child?

Once again, it all makes sense when Paul said how can you hold GOD's truth and walk in unrighteousness? You can't! Only true Believers hold GOD's truth and strive to walk in righteousness and live right. Not continue in their sin.

I don't see how people get this mixed up. Unless, they're trying to justify their sin. Verse 11, *And not only that, but we also rejoice in GOD through our Lord JESUS CHRIST, through whom we have now received reconciliation.* Do you know what the Biblical definition of reconciliation means? It means the process by which GOD and man are brought together again. According to verse 10, our sins made us enemies of GOD. JESUS' blood reconciled us back to GOD. You can't be reconciled if you are still considered an enemy. You can call yourself a sinner if you want to. I consider myself as the righteousness of GOD. As long as JESUS' blood covers me, when GOD sees me, HE doesn't see a sinner. Because of my faith, HE sees me as the righteousness of GOD.

Verse 19, *For as by one man's disobedience (Adam), many were made sinners. So, also by one Man's obedience (JESUS), many will be made righteous.* Interpretation: Because of Adam's sin, we all were considered sinners. And because of JESUS's obedience, those who are now Believers have been made righteous. Either you are still a sinner or you have been made righteous through JESUS' blood. You can't be both!

The only way a Believer can still call themselves a sinner is when they are trying to justify the sin they want to keep practicing. At that point, yes you are a sinner. If you are still a sinner, that means you are still an enemy to GOD. To call yourself a sinner says you have not been reconciled back to GOD. Sinners are not going to make it into heaven. Only those who have been reconciled through JESUS' blood. If you are a Believer that has been reconciled, stop calling yourself a sinner and start calling yourself the righteousness of GOD. I don't know about you, but I have been reconciled. I've been converted from a sinner and made the righteousness of GOD. My name is Melvin H. King, and I approve of this message!

A Comparison Between Adam & CHRIST
Verses 12-21

In verse 19, Paul tells us how we got the label of being a sinner. Through Adam's disobedience. Now, let's back up to verse 12. Paul does a comparison between Adam and CHRIST; *Sin came into the world through one person*, and that person was who? Adam. Because sin was birthed, *death came through sin. And so death passed upon all men, for that all have sinned.* When Adam sinned, it caused his blood to be tainted. Anything that comes from Adam, comes with tainted blood; sin.

When we were born, we were born with tainted blood which made us sinners. Sin brought death with it. Death was passed on to us because of Adam's sin. Because we were born with tainted blood, it gave us the nature to sin. That's why we all were considered sinners. We were born into it; we inherited it. Just because we inherited it, doesn't mean we have to keep it. No one was born righteous, except JESUS! HE was the only one that didn't have tainted blood.

Verses 13-14, *Sin was in the world before there were any laws. But no record of sin can be kept when there are no laws. Yet, death ruled from the time of Adam to the time of Moses, even over those who did not sin in the same way Adam did when he disobeyed. Adam is an image of the one who would come.*

In other words, Adam broke the covenant, but JESUS fixed the covenant. Adam destroyed the relationship between man and GOD. JESUS restored the relationship between man and GOD. What Adam broke, JESUS fixed. Adam established us as sinners. JESUS established us as the righteousness of GOD.

The danger of sin is, that sin doesn't come by itself. Verse 12 says it also comes with death. JESUS said the *thief comes to kill, steal, and destroy. But I came so that my sheep will have life...* (John 10:10) Do you see what the enemy did to Adam? He caused Adam to sin. Through sin, death came. JESUS says to us, "I come to restore what Adam broke and what the enemy killed, stole and destroyed."

Look at verse 13 again. *Sin was in the world before there were any laws. But no record of sin can be kept when there are no laws.* Here's how you know that we were born into sin. How do you all know that lying is a sin? We have GOD's Word that tells us. How do we know murder is a sin? We have GOD's Word that tells us.

So basically, we know when we have sinned when we have done something that GOD's Word tells us not to do. Paul said, "Even before there was a law to tell us what sin was, man sinned by nature." The reason I know driving 100 miles an hour is against the law is because the government has established a speed limit law. You have to be pretty corrupt to sin against GOD when there are no laws to establish what sin is.

That's why GOD was so hard on sin before the laws; man was sinning by nature. To sin by nature is to rebel against GOD. That's why we are considered enemies to GOD when we were sinners. In other words, it was a deep-rooted problem in man that caused man to disobey GOD. That problem disconnected us from GOD.

When JESUS died and man accepts JESUS' blood as their sacrifice, then grace steps in and fixes that deep-rooted problem in man's nature. Paul says "You can't hold GOD's truth and continue to also walk in unrighteousness" To walk in unrighteousness, is to continually walk in sin. I don't know about you, but I don't continually walk in sin. I may sin, but I don't continually walk in it. Paul said, "True Believers, even though they may sin, they don't continue in sin. They continue in *well-doing*.

Verses 15-17, *There is no comparison between GOD's gift and Adam's failure. For if by the one man's offense (Adam) many died, much more the grace of GOD and the gift by the grace of the one Man, JESUS CHRIST, abounded to many. There is also no comparison between GOD's gift and the one who sinned. The verdict which followed one person's failure condemned everyone. But, even after many failures, the gift brought GOD's approval. It is certain that death ruled because of one person's failure. It's even more certain that those who receive GOD's overflowing kindness and the gift of HIS approval will rule in life because of one person, JESUS CHRIST.*

If grace didn't step in and save us, then yes, we are still sinners and also an enemy to GOD. If grace has saved you, then those of us who have received this grace are going to reign in life with JESUS CHRIST. Look at what Paul says this type of approval by GOD is in verse 17. He says it's a gift of righteousness. Gifts are given freely. It only costs the giver, not the receiver.

Verses 18-19, *Therefore, as through one man's offense judgment came to all men, resulting in condemnation, even so through one Man's righteous act the free gift came to all men, resulting in justification of life. For as by one man's disobedience, many were made sinners, so also by one Man's obedience, many will be made righteous.* According to the text and not my interpretation or opinion, either you are a sinner or you have been made righteous. If I have been made righteous, why would I still consider myself a sinner?

Adam's sin brought us condemnation. GOD's gift brought us justification. Why would I still embrace condemnation after I have been justified? It kind of sounds like a trick of the enemy to me. If I continually consider myself a sinner, then I'll never continue in *well-doing*. What do sinners do? They sin. Those who have been made in the righteousness of GOD, what do they do? They continue in *well-doing*.

Verses 20 & 21, *Laws were added to increase the failure. But where sin increased, GOD's kindness increased even more.* Somebody say, no excuse! *As sin ruled by bringing death, GOD's kindness would rule by bringing us HIS approval. This results in our living forever because of JESUS CHRIST our Lord.*

It's only through the righteousness of JESUS CHRIST that we can enter into heaven and live forever. As Believers, we don't need an excuse for us to continue in sin by continuing to call ourselves sinners. We have been made the righteousness of GOD. Let the sinners continue to sin. Let the righteousness of GOD continue in *well-doing*. Because, *where sin increased, GOD's kindness increased even more*. There is absolutely no reason for us to continue to sin or call ourselves sinners.

Chapter 6
No Longer Slaves

No Longer Slaves to Sin, But GOD's Servants
Verses 1-23

Chapter 5 left off by talking about how we are no longer sinners, because we have been justified. Chapter 6 starts by reminding us that we are no longer slaves to sin, but we are now servants of GOD. Verses 1 and 2, *What should we say then? Should we continue to sin so that GOD's kindness will increase? That's unthinkable! As far as sin is concerned, we have died. So, how can we still live under sin's influence?*

Paul says, "If grace did its job, it's not even possible to be a practicing sinner." The moment we accepted CHRIST we died to sin. Sin no longer has influence over us. Look at what Paul says in verse 2, "To think that we can continue in sin after grace has stepped in and done its job is *unthinkable!*" The problem in the church is that a lot of people are trying to embrace salvation by dismissing the work of grace. You don't become saved until you have been delivered and freed from sin by grace. To be controlled by sin means you were never freed from sin. If salvation has taken place, there's no possible way to dismiss the work of grace.

That's why it's so hard to have this conversation about sin in the church, especially with so-called "Believers". They want to talk about the struggles of sin without discussing the work of grace. If we take the work of grace out of the conversation, it's easy for us to justify the sins we are committing. You can't discuss salvation and not talk about the work of grace. The Bible says *it is through grace that you are saved through faith!* (Ephesians 2:8) If grace doesn't step in, then we can't be saved.

It all makes sense. As a Believer, even though it is possible to sin, it is not possible to continue in sin. Why? Sin no longer has control, because it is now dead. Paul says in the next few verses, "People are making this way too difficult." The reason people are making this difficult is that either they're trying to justify their sins or they're trying to find out what sins they can continue to get away with.

Verses 3 and 4, *Don't you know that all of us who were baptized into CHRIST JESUS were baptized into His death? When we were baptized into His death, we were placed into the tomb with Him. As CHRIST was brought back from death to life by the glorious power of the FATHER, so we, too, should live a new kind of life.* In other words, Believers continue in well-doing. Sinners continue in their sin. Believers don't continue in sin. The only way to continue in sin is that grace never stepped in. To call yourself a sinner after grace has stepped in and made you the righteousness of GOD is an insult to the work that grace has done. Remember what Paul said earlier, "When we were sinners, we were enemies to GOD." My question is, how can you be saved, yet you are still an enemy to GOD? Back to verse 2. It's unthinkable!

In verses 5 through 7, Paul says, "It's not that difficult to understand." *If we've become united with Him in a death like His, certainly, we will also be united with Him when we come back to life as He did. We know that the person we used to be was crucified with Him to put an end to sin in our bodies. Because of this, we are no longer slaves to sin. The person who has died has been freed from sin.*

The only way I can misinterpret this passage of Scripture is because I'm trying to justify my sins. Paul makes it plain and simple in verse 6. He says, "We are no longer slaves to sin." Then verse 7 he says because *the person who has died has been freed from sin.* If I was once a slave, why would I still consider myself a slave after I have been freed from slavery? It doesn't make sense. The only way I would still consider myself a slave is, that I'm trying to convince others of the reason why I'm still working on Massah's plantation. Why would I still work on his plantation if I've been set free? If you are a Believer, that means, 'you's free!' You are no longer a slave to sin. If grace has saved you, trust and believe that you are truly free!

Now, being free doesn't stop you from having sin tendencies. That's why, as a Believer, you may still sin, because you have sin tendencies. As a Believer, you are no longer controlled by sin. Neither are you in bondage to sin. The moment you sin, the HOLY SPIRIT inside you will quickly remind you of what you just did is not right.

Watch how profound Paul makes this statement. He says, "How can GOD's grace set you free from bondage, but yet you are still in bondage? It's not possible." That's why he says in verse 2 GOD forbid. The only way you can still be in bondage is that you were never set free.

Our problem in the Body of CHRIST is that we think just because people are in church, they have been set free. There are a whole lot of people in the church that shout every Sunday and are still in bondage to sin. That's why they don't have a problem practicing it.

Being in church doesn't make you a Believer. Just like being in the garage doesn't make you a car. The bottom line is this, all Paul is saying here is, as a Believer, a true Believer, it is easier to strive to live right than it is to freely live in sin. The knowledge of your position as a Believer will always remind you WHO lives inside of you. To say that a Believer can continue in sin is just like saying GOD's grace encourages us to sin. How can I be a Believer that's been saved by grace, but my lifestyle resembles the lifestyle of a practicing sinner?

Verses 8-11, *If we have died with CHRIST, we believe that we will also live with Him. We know that CHRIST, who was brought back to life, will never die again. Death no longer has any power over Him. When He died, He died once and for all to sin's power. But now He lives, and He lives for GOD. So consider yourselves dead to sin's power but living for GOD in the power CHRIST JESUS gives you.*

To say that Believers can continue and practice sin is not only saying that GOD's grace encourages us to sin, but it reverses everything that took place in verses 8-11. In verse 9, Paul said, *death no longer has control over* CHRIST. When CHRIST died and was resurrected, HE took the power from death. That's why HE will never die again.

Verse 11 Paul says, "Likewise you also, because we are attached to Him and He is attached to us, we operate in the same dominion over sin that CHRIST operates in." If CHRIST is not a slave, I'm not a slave either. If CHRIST is not a sinner, I'm not a sinner, because I am connected to Him through HIS blood. When GOD sees me, HE sees HIS Son JESUS.

Sin has to respect you, because of Who you are connected to. Demonic spirits have to respect you, because of Who you are connected to. That's why sinners can't make you do anything. They can only influence you to do it. Why? They no longer have dominion over you. You have dominion over sin.

To show you that we have dominion and control over sin, look at what Paul says in verse 12. *Therefore, never let sin rule your physical body so that you obey its desires.* The keywords in verse 12 are *let* and *obey*. Paul says don't *let* sin control you. The only way sin can control you now is that you have to *let* it control you. You have to choose to *obey* it.

My question is, why *obey* something that has no power? Why *let* something have power over you that you have power over? If I am a true Believer that has power over sin, I can never say that sin took control of me. The real reason is that I *let* sin have its way. I allowed sin to influence my flesh. I can't even use the excuse, 'It was a struggle.'

Verses 13-14, *And do not present your members as instruments of unrighteousness to sin, but present yourselves to GOD as being alive from the dead, and your members as instruments of righteousness to GOD. For sin shall not have dominion over you, for you are not under law but under grace.*

How can something I have dominion over be a struggle? Unless we share the same power. You cannot share the same power with something you have dominion over. For people who try to justify their lifestyle of sin, here's the real issue, they were never set free. Grace is not going to set us free from sin for us to walk around in bondage.

When we look at verse 15, Paul is thinking hard about this issue. He sort of asked the same question in verse 15 that he asks in verses 1 and 2. Now, if Paul had to ask the same question twice and still came up with the same answer, twice, basically what Paul is saying is, "There is no excuse. Stop trying to come up with one!"

Look at what he says in verse 15. *What then? Shall we sin because we are not under law but now under grace?* Once again he says, certainly not! Wow!!! That's powerful!

How can grace encourage you to participate in something GOD freed you from? That's why it's so hard to have this conversation with people. To have this conversation means you might have to admit that you might not be saved. So, instead of admitting that there is a possibility that they are not saved, they have to try to justify why they are still practicing sin and also saved by grace. Which Paul says is impossible!

The mistake that people continue to make in the Body of CHRIST, even today, is that they try to convince the world that even though they were saved by grace, somehow they are still in bondage to sin even though we now have control over sin.

Look at how Paul responds to this way of thinking in verse 16. *Don't you know that if you offer to be someone's slave, you must obey that master? Either your master is sin, or your master is obedience. Letting sin be your master leads to death. Letting obedience be your master leads to GOD's approval.* I don't think Paul could have made it any simpler than this. This eliminates any excuse I can come up with to justify my lifestyle of sin. If I have been truly saved by grace, I have control and dominion over sin; any sin!

Verse 17, *You were slaves to sin. But I thank GOD that you have become wholeheartedly obedient to the teachings which you were given.* Because of the teachings that you were giving, Paul says in verse 18, *And having been set free from sin, you became slaves of righteousness.* How can you work for righteousness and continue to work for sin for free? The wages for righteousness are eternal life. The wages of sin is death.

That's why I stated before that if you have been truly delivered and saved by grace, it should be easier to strive to live righteously than it is to live a lifestyle of sin. Look at what happens in verse 18 to those who have been set free. They are no longer slaves to sin, but they now became slaves of righteousness. They switch owners. Each owner has their requirements. There is no way you can tell me that you are a slave of righteousness, but it's easier to live a lifestyle of sin. That's why Paul says both times, that's unthinkable!

In verse 19 Paul says, "When you were sinners, it was easy to offer your body to sin. Why? You were a slave to it. It controlled you." Verse 19, *I'm speaking in a human way because of the weakness of your corrupt nature. Clearly, you once offered all the parts of your body as slaves to sexual perversion and disobedience. This led you to live disobedient lives. Now, in the same way, offer all the parts of your body as slaves that do what GOD approves of. This leads you to live holy lives.*

Paul says, "When grace delivered you, you became a slave to righteousness. It leads you to live a holy life." That's why when you have truly been saved, even though this testimony is most quoted, it has some truth to it; That things I used to do I don't do anymore. Places I used to go, I don't go anymore. Why? Once you have been made the righteousness of GOD, it's easier to strive to live right than it is to live wrong. Grace doesn't make you sinless. It should cause you to sin less. Just as easy as it was to sin before you got saved, now that you are saved, it should be that easier to live right. If someone finds living right a struggle, it's probably because they are not saved.

I just have to be honest, before I became saved, even though I wasn't a bad person when I did wrong, I didn't consider my wrong-doing as wrong. Which caused me to freely do wrong without the thought of it being wrong. Now that I am saved and GOD's SPIRIT dwells in me, I have to think about doing wrong. I have to choose if I'm going to give in to the desires of my flesh. When I have a thought about doing wrong, immediately, the SPIRIT quickens me and reminds me that what I am thinking about doing is wrong.

Once the SPIRIT reminds me that what I'm thinking is wrong, then HE says to me, "Now, what are you going to do?" Trust me, it's harder to go through with what I was thinking than it is to give in to my flesh. Why? Because, the desires of my flesh no longer have control over me even though my flesh may still have desires.

If you truly have the HOLY SPIRIT inside of you, it convicts you at the thought of doing wrong. We decide whether to go through with it or not. If you choose to go through with it, the SPIRIT inside of you causes you to feel bad afterward because you were first convicted at the thought of doing wrong. Because of the double conviction, the thought, and the act, it causes you to go into repentance. You knew you were wrong after the thought. That's only if you are truly saved. Sinners are not convicted at the thought or the action. Actually, sinners find satisfaction in the thought and the action of giving in to the flesh.

Why? The flesh will always find satisfaction with sin because it was born into it. That's why it takes GOD's SPIRIT of conviction to correct us at the thought of sin. If someone can sin without thought or conviction and it's easier to sin than it is to live right, then they need to ask themselves, "Who's my master?"

Paul says in verse 18, once you were freed from sin, *you became slaves of righteousness.* Satan is the master of sin. GOD is the MASTER of righteousness. Once again, who is your master? I think Elijah said it best when he asks GOD's people in 1 Kings 18:21 *How long will you try to have it both ways? If the LORD is GOD, follow HIM; if Baal is god, follow him.*

Verse 20, *When you were slaves to sin, you were free from doing what GOD approves of.* WOW! That's powerful! Here's when you know who you belong to. When you feel free to do whatever you choose to do, and if you feel free to sin, then you are still a slave to sin and sin is your master. If you feel free to live right, then you are a slave to righteousness and GOD is your MASTER. It's just that simple! So, let me ask you again, "Who's yo daddy/master?"

To back-up everything that was just mentioned, verses 21 through 23 tell us exactly who our DADDY and MASTER is. Verses 21, *What did you gain by doing those things? You're ashamed of what you used to do, because it ended in death.* Not only should sin convict you at the thought of it, but it should make you feel ashamed. Why? Because you know GOD is looking at you shaking HIS head in disappointment. That's why when David sinned with Bathsheba, David felt bad and went before GOD and said, *Against you, you only, have I sinned and done what is evil in your sight;...* (Psalm 51:4 NIV)

David didn't feel ashamed for sinning against himself. He didn't feel ashamed, because he sinned with Bathsheba. David didn't even feel the shame of his sin, because he slept with someone else's wife. David felt ashamed because he knew he had sinned against GOD.

Verses 22 and 23, *Now you have been freed from sin and have become GOD's slaves. This results in a holy life and, finally, in everlasting life. The payment for sin is death, but the gift that GOD freely gives is everlasting life found in CHRIST JESUS our Lord.* Now, that we have been delivered and set free, we work for righteousness. Our payment is eternal life with GOD. It doesn't make any sense to work for GOD, but our payment is death.

Either we are still sinners, or we have been made the righteousness of GOD. We can't be both! You can't be a righteous sinner!

I don't know about you, but I would rather become GOD's slave than sin's whore! Leviticus 19:29 (KJV), *Do not prostitute your daughter, to cause her to be a whore; lest the land fall to whoredom, and the land become full of wickedness.* The payment that sin and wickedness give for prostituting us is death. GOD gives us everlasting life.

Chapter 7
Moses' Laws

The Reality of The Law & The Flesh
Verses 1-6

In Chapter 7, Paul continues the conversation about sin from chapter 6. He is trying to explain and bring clarity to this issue of sin. Evidently, he knew that this was going to be a problem. I like how Paul deals with the issue of sin in chapter 7. He deals with the reality of The Law and the reality of the flesh. Even though Paul deals with the reality of them both, they still should never contradict themselves.

We must get clarity on this sin problem, because Chapter 7 is one of the most misinterpreted passages of Scriptures that people try to use to justify their sinful behavior. At the end of chapter 7, verses 15 through 17, Paul makes a statement by saying, *what I know to do, I don't do. And what I know not to do, that's what I do. And it's all because of the sin that dwells in me.* People quote that passage as if that gives them an excuse to sin. So, let's get some clarity out of Romans chapter 7 so the next time you hear somebody try to justify their lifestyle of sin, you'll know how to correct them.

In chapter 7, it is almost as if Paul is saying, "I have dealt with the spiritual aspect of what took place in the spirit because of sin and you understand it. Now, let's deal with the reality of it all." Look at how he starts off chapter 7 in verse 1. Paul says, "For those of you that know The Law, let's deal with the reality of The Law first." *Don't you realize, brothers and sisters, that laws have power over people only as long as they are alive? (I'm speaking to people who are familiar with Moses' Teachings.)*

It's obvious Paul has something up his sleeve. Paul knew, if they didn't understand anything else, he knew they understood The Law. If they didn't understand GOD's Word, they understood Moses's Law. So, he says, "As long as you are living, you're going to have to deal with laws. The only time laws do not affect you is when you're dead. Then you are no longer required to keep The Law."

The message that Paul is trying to get them to understand is, that dead people are free from The Law. The Law has no power or jurisdiction over someone who is dead. You can't expect a dead person to follow The Law. Why? They are no longer living.

Then Paul gives them an example to help them better understand verses 2 and 3. *For example, a married woman is bound by law to her husband as long as he is alive. But if her husband dies, that marriage law is no longer in effect for her. So, if she marries another man while her husband is still alive, she will be called an adulterer. But if her husband dies, she is free from this law, so she is not committing adultery if she marries another man.*

Let's look at the two positions that Paul explains to them about The Law. The first one is, that if you are living, you are required to follow The Law. You can't be expected to follow The Law if you are dead. The second position is, that death frees you from The Law. When a person dies, they are no longer under The Law, and neither can they be condemned by The Law. After Paul explains to them about a dead man being free from The Law, he then hits them with verse 4. *In the same way, brothers and sisters, you have died to the laws in Moses' Teachings through CHRIST's body. You belong to someone else, the one who was brought back to life. As a result, we can do what GOD wants.*

Watch what Paul says, "As a sinner, you are required to follow the Mosaic Law. If you are required to follow the Mosaic Law, then the Mosaic Law has every right to condemn and judge you if you break its law." The moment the sinner in you died and grace made you the righteousness of GOD, you died to the Mosaic Law. Just like a dead man is not required or expected to follow The Law, as a born-again Believer, you are not required to follow the Mosaic Law. That Law was for the sinner and not the redeemed righteous.

The redeemed righteous person is no longer bound by those laws, because now they are covered under grace. To call yourself a sinner means you have to follow every one of the Mosaic Laws. If you are bound by those laws, if you choose to break any of those laws, you should be condemned and judged by those laws. I thank GOD that I am free from condemnation. Romans 8:1 says, *Therefore, there is no condemnation for those who are in CHRIST JESUS.* Which we'll talk more about in the next chapter.

Grace steps in and says, "For you to be set free, the sinner person has to die. When you are serious about allowing the sinner to die, here's what I'm going to do. I'm going to cover you with grace. So that way when GOD sees you, HE doesn't see the sinner, but HE sees the righteousness of HIS Son JESUS." That's why Paul said we have been made into the righteousness of GOD. To dismiss the work of grace, just to justify your lifestyle is to be bound by the Mosaic Law. I don't know about you, but I would rather be covered by grace than be a slave to The Law.

Here's what The Law did in verses 5 and 6. *While we were living under the influence of our corrupt nature, sinful passions were at work throughout our bodies. Stirred up by Moses' Laws, our sinful passions did things that result in death. But now, we have died to those laws that bound us. GOD has broken their effect on us so that we are serving in a new spiritual way, not in an old way dictated by written words.*

As I said, I would rather be under grace than bound by The Law or a law. Under The Law, The Law caused our nature to be sinful. The punishment of sin is death. That's why Paul said in chapter 6, for the wages of sin is, what? Death! But the gift of GOD is eternal life. The reason grace freed us from The Law is that GOD looked at The Law and said, "The only thing The Law is doing is bringing condemnation, punishment, discouragement and a sense of disappointment. So, GOD said, "Let ME send MY Son, so whosoever believes in HIM should not be in bondage to The Law and will not perish because of The Law, but have everlasting life.

Moses' Laws Show What Sin Is
Verses 7-13

Verse 7, *What should we say, then? Are Moses' laws sinful?* Paul, are you telling us that Moses's laws are sinful? Paul says, "That's unthinkable! In fact, I wouldn't have recognized sin if those laws hadn't shown it to me. For example, I wouldn't have known that some desires are sinful if Moses' Teachings hadn't said, 'Never have wrong desires.'" Paul says the benefit of Moses' Laws was that they caused us to recognize what was wrong. The problem with pointing out everything wrong is, because of our sinful nature, the moment you bring what we're not supposed to do to our attention, it causes us to want to do it. The Law did more damage than it did good. Instead of it reminding us not to sin, it caused us to sin.

Think about it. When the Mosaic Laws were created, they were intended to bring the people closer to GOD. Instead, it brought the people further away from GOD. The Mosaic Law ended up replacing GOD. GOD is a GOD of freedom. Everything about HIM represents freedom. Instead of The Laws that were established to represent GOD to bring us freedom, it put us in bondage. Not only did it put us in bondage, but The Laws brought us condemnation.

Paul explains how all this happened in verses 8 through 11. *But sin took the opportunity provided by this commandment and made me have all kinds of wrong desires. Clearly, without laws, sin is dead. At one time I was alive without any laws. But when this commandment came, sin became alive and I died. I found that the commandment which was intended to bring me life actually brought me death. Sin, taking the opportunity provided by this commandment, deceived me and then killed me.*

Instead of The Law helping us, sin took The Law and caused the same thing that was supposed to help us to hurt us. The same thing that was supposed to bring us liberty brought us misery and put us in bondage. Paul says in verse 12. *So Moses' Teachings are holy, and the commandment is holy, right, and good.* Now, look at what Paul says in verse 13, because you know it was going to be somebody that would ask this question. *Now, did something good cause my death? That's unthinkable! Rather, my death was caused by sin so that sin would be recognized for what it is. Through a commandment, sin became more sinful than ever.* Instead of The Law reminding us not to sin, sin took The Law and caused us to become more sinful than ever.

GOD's Standards Are at War With Sin's Standards
Verses 14-25

Not only did sin take The Law and caused us to become more sinful, along with bondage, it also brought condemnation. Think about it, in the Old Testament, they would stone and punish you. Sometimes, they put you to death if you broke The Law. GOD never intended for man to become a judge using The Law.

Even in the New Testament, the Pharisees kept trying to find ways to prove JESUS broke The Law just so they could put Him to death. They took The Law to condemn Him. The Law was never supposed to bring condemnation. That's why grace had to step in to replace The Law and defend us from it. Grace is not going to set you free from something for you to walk around and continue to be in bondage to it.

Remember what The Law was designed to do, guide and direct you, and to remind and make us aware of what we should not do. According to verse 13, sin took The Law, and instead of The Law guiding us and directing us, it gave man the power to judge and then turn around and persecute us. Sin became more sinful from The Law. Along with sin came death. As a sinner, not only were we in bondage by The Law, but we were also in bondage to sin. The penalty for sin is death.

For five chapters, that's what Paul has been teaching us. Not only does grace free us from The Law, but it also frees us from sin. We are no longer in bondage to The Law or sin. Here's where this passage gets misinterpreted. We must understand what Paul is saying. When you read verses 14 through

20, it sounds like Paul contradicts everything he taught us about freedom.

I know that GOD's standards are spiritual, but I have a corrupt nature, sold as a slave to sin. I don't realize what I'm doing. I don't do what I want to do. Instead, I do what I hate. I don't do what I want to do, but I agree that GOD's standards are good. So, I am no longer the one who is doing the things I hate, but the sin that lives in me is doing them. I know that nothing good lives in me; that is, nothing good lives in my corrupt nature. Although I have the desire to do what is right, I don't do it. I don't do the good I want to do. Instead, I do the evil that I don't want to do. Now, when I do what I don't want to do, I am no longer the one who is doing it. Sin that lives in me is doing it.

Paul has been talking about the work of grace. How grace freed us from sin. By us being freed from sin, we now have dominion over sin. Now, here in verses 14 – 20, it almost sounds like he's talking as if he doesn't have any control over what his corrupt nature does. Look at what Paul says, "That which I know not to do, because of sin, which I am supposed to have control over causes me to sin."

Then he says, "That which I know to do, because of sin which I am supposed to have control over, I don't do. The reason I don't do what I'm supposed to do and do what I'm not supposed to do, is because of the sin that dwells in me." If you study this passage of Scripture wrong, you would think that either Paul is contradicting himself or we as Believers are still in bondage to sin. I have heard people teach about the corrupt nature and its faults more than I have heard them teach about us having dominion over sin. Every time they want to justify their sins, they always talk about Romans chapter 7 verses 14 through 20.

Let's understand what Paul is saying. If you don't read the whole text, then it sounds like Paul is saying we don't have control over our corrupt nature, but sin does. If that was the case, what was the purpose of grace? For me to say I have been saved by grace, but yet, I am still in bondage to sin, is an insult to GOD. Because now, I'm saying that sin has more power than GOD's grace. As if, what took place at the cross wasn't powerful enough to defeat sin. We know that's a lie! Let's read and understand the text in its entirety so we can get a full understanding.

Now, remember, we talked about being free from sin doesn't stop you from having sin tendencies. That's why, as a Believer, you may sin. Even as a Believer, you still have and will have sin tendencies. Believers are no longer controlled by sin. Neither are we in bondage to sin. The difference between a Believer and a sinner is, a Believer continues in well-doing, and a sinner continues in their sins.

That's why GOD placed HIS HOLY SPIRIT inside of us because HE knew the flesh carried the tendency to sin. The moment we sin, the HOLY SPIRIT inside of us quickly reminds us what we just did was wrong. What we did violated GOD's standards. Thank GOD for having the HOLY SPIRIT.

What is Paul saying in verses 14 – 20? Why do so many Believers run to Romans chapter 7 verses 14 through 22 to try and explain their sinful nature as if this verse justifies us being righteous sinners? Let's get some understanding of this matter by starting with verse 14. *I know that GOD's standards are spiritual, but I have a corrupt nature, sold as a slave to sin.* Paul says, "Regardless of what my flesh does and regardless of my sinful nature, GOD's standards are always spiritual and right." Let's erase that excuse right now. If I mess up, I can't blame it on GOD. The problem is always my flesh.

After Paul erases the excuses of trying to blame GOD, he then starts talking about why we do what we know we shouldn't be doing. The reason we do what we shouldn't be doing or we don't do what we know we should be doing is because of our corrupt nature. "Hold up! Paul, I thought we were no longer in bondage to our corrupt nature." We're not! But, because we were born with a sinful nature, and even being freed from sin and saved by grace, the flesh still tends to sin.

As a matter of fact, every now and then our flesh wants to sin. You would be deceiving yourself if you thought differently. The only difference now is, that the flesh is no longer controlled by sin. Sin no longer has control over our flesh. We have control over sin, even if our flesh still wants it.

That's the danger for a lot of Believers. They think that just because they have been saved, they no longer have sin tendencies. Every time they have a bad thought, they feel like they have to get resaved again. They think that falling short is a sign of not being saved.

When Believers feel that having tendencies to sin means we're not saved, instead of us trying to restore each other, we end up trying to rebaptize each other. Not realizing that all of us have sin tendencies in the flesh. We become judgmental and try to hide our sin tendencies so we can be judgmental regarding others' sins. That's why Paul said, as Believers, we strive to live righteously. When we do fall short, we continue in *well-doing*. What made us fall short? Our tendency to sin.

There's one verse that makes sense of all of this. Look at verse 21. I find; I discovered. Because of what I have discovered, I am now aware, that, when I would do good, evil is present with me. Not that it causes me to do evil, but it causes me to be aware of my sin tendencies. What do sin tendencies tend to do? Sin. Paul says when you are aware of what your flesh wants, even though you are saved, sanctified, filled with the HOLY SPIRIT, been saved by grace, and sin no longer has control over you, your flesh still tends to want to sin.

When you are aware that your flesh wants to sin, it's easier for you to check your flesh and tell your flesh, "no" than it is to go through with the sin. In Verses 22 – 24, Paul says *I take pleasure in GOD's standards in my inner being. However, I see a different standard at work throughout my body. It is at war with the standards my mind sets and tries to take me captive to sin's standards which still exist throughout my body. What a miserable person I am! Who will rescue me from my dying body?*

As Believers, we need to always be aware that our tendency to sin will always be at war with what we know is right. At first, when our mind and our flesh were corrupt, we had an excuse to sin. Now, that GOD has renewed our minds and we are no longer in bondage, we have the choice to sin. The choice to sin and the choice to live right will always be at war with our flesh.

The advantage the choice to sin has over the choice to live right is, that the choice to sin knows that the flesh wants to sin. That's why Paul said in verse 24 *O wretched man that I am!* Who will deliver me from this body of death? In other words, this body that wants to sin. Even when my flesh is struggling with the two choices, look at what Paul says in verse 25. *I thank GOD through JESUS CHRIST our Lord. So, then with the mind, I myself serve the law of GOD; but with the flesh the law of sin.*

At first, it was an uneven match; I had two choices. The first choice is to sin, the second choice is to live right. If my flesh has sin tendencies, then guess what my flesh wants to do? It wants to choose to sin. Paul says, to make the match a fair fight, we can thank GOD who sent us HIS Son JESUS and the HOLY SPIRIT to help us to choose to live right. That's an even match.

Chapter 8
GOD's SPIRIT

GOD's SPIRIT Makes Us HIS Children
Verses 1-17

Chapter 8 opens up by letting us know that we are no longer under The Law that condemns us. Sin took The Law and caused man to sin against GOD. Even in the Garden of Eden, Satan took GOD's command and used it against man and made us go against GOD's command.

Genesis 3:1-6, The snake was more clever than all the wild animals the LORD GOD had made. He asked the woman, "Did GOD really say, 'You must never eat the fruit of any tree in the garden'?" The woman answered the snake, "We're allowed to eat the fruit from any tree in the garden except the tree in the middle of the garden. GOD said, 'You must never eat it or touch it. If you do, you will die!'" "You certainly won't die!" the snake told the woman. "GOD knows that when you eat it your eyes will be opened. You'll be like GOD, knowing good and evil." The woman saw that the tree had fruit that was good to eat, nice to look at, and desirable for making someone wise. So, she took some of the fruit and ate it. She also gave some to her husband, who was with her, and he ate it.

That's why grace stepped in, replaced The Law, and defended us from The Law. A lot of people have this confused. We are no longer under man's laws to make us acceptable to GOD. We are under GOD's Law and that's the Law of Grace. Even though grace freed us from the condemnation of The Law, grace still has some requirements. Most people want to treat grace as if it doesn't require us to do anything. Just because we are under grace doesn't mean we can do anything we like. When grace set us free from The

Law, not only did it set us free from The Law, but it also freed us from sin. We are no longer in bondage to The Law or sin. Since we are no longer in bondage to either, then we are not supposed to practice either. By us being under grace, we're not supposed to practice The Law and neither are we supposed to practice sin.

Verse 1, *So those who are Believers in CHRIST JESUS can no longer be condemned.* Did y'all see what Paul just said? I can't be condemned by something I'm no longer required to follow. Look at what Paul continues to say in verse 2. *The standards of the SPIRIT, who gives life through CHRIST JESUS, have set you free from the standards of sin and death.* Wow!! That's powerful. GOD's Word doesn't contradict itself. I like how it validates itself.

Verse 3-4, *It is impossible to do what GOD's standards demand because of the weakness our human nature has. But GOD sent HIS Son to have a human nature as sinners have and to pay for sin. That way GOD condemned sin in our corrupt nature. Therefore, we, who do not live by our corrupt nature, but by our spiritual nature, are able to meet GOD's standards.*

Verses 3 and 4 tell us there are two natures. The sinful corrupt nature which we were freed from and the Spiritual nature which we were delivered into. Because we were born with a corrupt nature, it always wants to participate in the evil around us. Verse 4 says *we do not live by our corrupt nature* but we live *by our Spiritual nature.* When we were in bondage to our corrupt nature, we didn't have a choice. Now, because of our Spiritual nature, which has been saved by grace, we *are able to meet GOD's standards* by choosing to live right. When grace does its job, it's easier for us to live right than it is for us to live wrong. Why? We are no longer in bondage to our corrupt nature.

I can't use the fact that because sin is present it causes me to sin, because Paul said, "I shouldn't be living by my corrupt nature anyway." Guess what our sin tendencies are going to want to follow? Our corrupt nature. Our corrupt nature and our Spiritual nature are going to always be at war with each other. You have to make the ultimate decision about which nature you're going to choose to follow. It shouldn't be a struggle to follow your Spiritual nature, because grace gave us the power over our corrupt nature.

Whenever we participate in and choose to sin, it's because we chose to follow our corrupt nature. Why follow something that no longer has power over you? It's the corrupt nature that tries to keep man separated from GOD through sin. The corrupt nature knows that sin separates us from GOD. Remember what Romans 8:35 says. *What shall separate us from the love of GOD?* If I have been saved by grace, it won't be my corrupt nature. Why? I have dominion over my corrupt nature.

The danger of living by a corrupt nature, verse 5 says *Those who live by the corrupt nature have the corrupt nature's attitude. But those who live by the spiritual nature have the spiritual nature's attitude.* One thing is for sure, you can't live by a corrupted nature and have a Spiritual mind. Neither can you live by a Spiritual nature and have a corrupt mind. Verse 6, *The corrupt nature's attitude leads to death. But the Spiritual nature's attitude leads to life and peace.* Why would I choose death when I have been given life and peace? How can anyone justify practicing any sin? Unless they don't want to admit they chose to follow their corrupt nature.

In verses 7-9, Paul breaks it down. *This is so because the corrupt nature has a hostile attitude toward GOD. It refuses to place itself under the authority of GOD's standards because it can't. Those who are under the control of the corrupt nature can't please GOD. But if GOD's Spirit lives in you, you are under the control of your Spiritual nature, not your corrupt nature.* It doesn't get any simpler than this. If it looks like sin, continues in sin, acts like sin, and always participates in sin, I can almost guarantee they haven't been saved by grace.

Anyone who is always guided by their corrupt nature, the reason it's such a fight for them to live right is because it's hard for them to place themselves under GOD's authority. There is no way I can be saved by grace, but I have a problem placing myself under GOD's authority. Verse 9 says GOD's SPIRIT lives in us. Because of HIS SPIRIT, *we are under the control of our spiritual nature.* It should never be a struggle to obey our Spiritual nature.

Here's how you can tell if someone is truly saved. Just see which nature they choose to live by. Verses 10-12, *However, if CHRIST lives in you, your bodies are dead because of sin, but your spirits are alive because you have GOD's approval. Does the SPIRIT of the one who brought JESUS back to life live in you? Then the one who brought CHRIST back to life will also make your mortal bodies alive by HIS SPIRIT who lives in you. So, brothers and sisters, we have no obligation to live the way our corrupt nature wants us to live.*

When you have been saved by grace, you don't have a choice but to live by your Spiritual nature. Even if you do have sin tendencies. It should be easier to strive to live right than it is to voluntarily choose to live wrong. We have dominion and authority over our corrupt nature. It no longer has the authority to tell us what to do. We have the authority to tell our corrupt nature what we're not going to do! That's why Paul says in 1st Corinthians 9:27, *I discipline my body and bring it into subjection.* My body doesn't tell me what to do. I have the authority to tell it what to do.

Verse 13 (NKJV), *For if you live according to the flesh you will die; but if by the SPIRIT you put to death the deeds of the body, you will live.* Once again, our corrupt nature doesn't have control over us. We have control over it. The danger of allowing our flesh to control us is, that it brings death. If we allow our Spiritual nature to control our corrupt nature; our flesh, Paul said, *you will live.*

Verses 14 – 17, *Certainly, all who are guided by GOD's SPIRIT are GOD's children. You haven't received the SPIRIT of slaves that leads you into fear again. Instead, you have received the SPIRIT of GOD's adopted children by which we call out, "Abba! Father!" The SPIRIT Himself testi-*

fies with our Spirit that we are GOD's children. If we are HIS children, we are also GOD's heirs. If we share in CHRIST's suffering in order to share His glory, we are heirs together with Him.

Verses 14 through 17 lets us know that we belong to GOD. As a matter of fact, we are HIS children. Because we are HIS children, being HIS child comes with benefits. Verse 17 says *we are heirs* and joint-heirs with CHRIST. What do you think are the benefits we receive by being heirs? Authority. Look at verse 14 again. *For you did not receive the SPIRIT of bondage again to fear, but you received the SPIRIT of adoption.* Because we have been adopted, our body then becomes a temple. GOD who is now our FATHER resides in our temple. If GOD SPIRIT resides and lives inside of us, how is it even possible for us to still be in bondage to our corrupt nature? It's not possible!

That's why I have authority. How and why do I have authority? Because, the GOD that lives in me gives me authority. As long as GOD is with me, I have authority. When GOD is not with me, I don't! Paul said, "You can't have GOD's SPIRIT, but yet, you are always controlled by your corrupt nature.

To say that GOD is in you, but yet, sin still controls you, means that sin is more powerful than the GOD that's in you." How can someone have GOD in them and they're always having an issue with sin? It's not possible! Verse 14 says those who are GOD's children are led by HIS SPIRIT. It's HIS SPIRIT that puts to death the flesh. I can't say I'm being led by the SPIRIT, but yet, I'm always being controlled by my flesh.

GOD's SPIRIT Helps Us
Verses 18-27

Verse 14 validates what verse 4 said. Look at what verse 4 has already told us. *Therefore, we do not live by our corrupt nature but we live by our Spiritual nature,...* Now, watch what Paul says in verses 18 – 22. *I consider our present sufferings insignificant compared to the glory that will soon be revealed to us. All creation is eagerly waiting for GOD to reveal who HIS children are. Creation was subjected to frustration but not by its own choice. The one who subjected it to frustration did so in the hope that it would also be set free from slavery to decay in order to share the glorious freedom that the children of GOD will have. We know that all creation has been groaning with the pains of childbirth up to the present time.*

Remember, we talked about having a corrupt nature and a Spiritual nature. These two will always be at war with one another. It's our choice to follow the Spiritual nature and be blessed or to be bamboozled by the corrupt nature and deal with the consequences. Even though we have authority over the corrupt nature, Paul is saying to us, it's still going to be a struggle. Why is it going to be a struggle? The flesh is going to always want to follow the corrupt nature. Sin tendencies are going to always want to sin.

Even though we have authority over our flesh, doesn't mean that it doesn't want to sin. We just have the authority to tell our flesh, "No." I may tell my children they can't go to the park. That doesn't mean they don't want to go. I just have the authority to tell them "No."

Paul is saying, "Even though we have authority over our sinful nature, doesn't mean it doesn't still want to sin."

Verse 23, *However, not only creation groans. We, who have the SPIRIT as the first of GOD's gifts, also groan inwardly. We groan as we eagerly wait for our adoption, the freeing of our bodies from sin.* Whenever the flesh has a sinful desire, the SPIRIT inside of us groans. In other words, it becomes disturbed. The SPIRIT knows our flesh is about to take advice from our corrupt nature. Our flesh is about to give authority to something that no longer has authority.

Whenever we allow sin to have authority over our flesh, it disturbs the HOLY SPIRIT inside of us who has given us power over our flesh. Which is sort of like an insult to the HOLY SPIRIT. If GOD's SPIRIT lives in me, it's no longer just me. It is now us. When I give sin authority, I'm not giving it authority over me, but I'm giving it authority over 'us'; me and the HOLY SPIRIT.

That's why the HOLY SPIRIT grieves when we participate in sin. The HOLY SPIRIT says, "I have authority over this. But, you have allowed sin to have authority over us." The HOLY SPIRIT has the power and the authority to make us choose to do what's right. The SPIRIT says if I have to make you choose to do what's right, then I have just tampered with your free-will ability to choose.

Verse 24, *We were saved with this hope in mind.* What hope, Paul? Go back to verse 23. *We groan as we eagerly wait for our adoption, the freeing of our bodies from sin*; the struggle in our flesh. Verse 24 goes on to say *If we hope for something we already see, then it's not really hope. Who hopes for what can be seen? But if we hope for what we don't see, we eagerly wait for it with perseverance.*

In other words, one day it won't be a struggle. GOD will eventually get rid of the corrupt nature. As long as we have options, GOD knew because of our sin tendencies, even though we have authority over our flesh, there were going to be times we would give in to the flesh. No matter how saved you are. No matter how big your Bible is. Even though we have authority over sin, eventually we're going to give sin authority over our flesh.

Verses 26 and 27, *At the same time the SPIRIT also helps us in our weakness, because we don't know how to pray for what we need. But the SPIRIT intercedes along with our groans that cannot be expressed in words. The one who searches our hearts knows what the SPIRIT has in mind. The SPIRIT intercedes for GOD's people the way GOD wants HIM to.*

Here's one of my favorite verses regarding the HOLY SPIRIT that dwells inside of us. Look at what Paul says in verse 26 *at the same time*. In that moment of weakness, the SPIRIT doesn't just give up on us. What did Paul say the SPIRIT do? HE helps us in our times of weakness. HE doesn't abandon us, but HE helps us.

Verse 26 says, even when we don't know what to pray for, verse 27 comes in and says, the HOLY SPIRIT inside of us intercedes on our behalf. When our flesh is saying, "I desire this," The HOLY SPIRIT says, "Yes, I know he wants that, but he doesn't need that." While our flesh is saying, "Please make a way for me to get it," the HOLY SPIRIT is saying, "Block her from getting it."

Look what the SPIRIT is doing just to keep us out of trouble. HE's groaning. HE is interceding. HE is making intercession. In other words, HE is laboring on our behalf. Could you imagine if the SPIRIT wasn't laboring on our behalf? We would be a train wreck waiting to happen. That's why I say, there's no way you can be saved by grace and be comfortable practicing sin. The HOLY SPIRIT is working too hard for you to not be comfortable.

If someone is comfortable practicing sin, it's because they don't have the HOLY SPIRIT. There is no way you can be comfortable living in sin and the HOLY SPIRIT is groaning, interceding, making intercession and you do not feel any guilt.

That's why when you commit any sin, you feel guilt after the sin has been committed. That is the laboring the HOLY SPIRIT was doing on your behalf. As long as you feel the guilt and the shame, you know that the HOLY SPIRIT is present. If you don't feel any guilt or shame (not condemnation) after giving in to sin, then that means the SPIRIT isn't present.

Nothing Can Separate Us from GOD's Love
Verses 28-39

The next few verses assure us that because GOD is with us, HE will never leave us. That's good to know, because most people feel that the minute you fall short GOD is no longer with you. As a matter of fact, the devil wants you to believe that when you fall short GOD is no longer with you. If I feel GOD is no longer with me, it causes me to continue in my sin. It hinders me from continuing in *well-doing*. Paul says in verse 28, the good news is, *We know that all things work together for the good...* even when I fall short. If I decide to get back up and *continue in well-doing*, it's going to work out for my good.

Look at what the text continues to say. It works out for *those who love GOD. Those whom HE has called according to HIS plan.* HIS plan for us is greater than our mistakes. HIS plan is greater than our struggles. HIS plan is greater than our weaknesses. GOD says, "I have to help you in your time of weakness, because MY plan is greater than your weakness".

That's why it's important that we follow our Spiritual nature and not our corrupt nature. Anytime we give authority to our corrupt nature, we are affecting HIS plan. GOD says, "That's why I'M giving you authority over your corrupt nature. MY plan is greater than the desires of your flesh. That's why you are no longer under The Law, but now under grace. MY plan is greater than The Law." Anything that will put you in bondage, GOD says, "I have given you authority over it, because MY plan is greater."

Verse 29-30, *This is true because HE already knew HIS people and had already appointed them to have the same form as the image of HIS Son. Therefore, HIS Son is the firstborn among many children. HE also called those whom HE had already appointed. HE approved of those whom HE had called, and HE gave glory to those whom HE had approved of.*

See, how all this is coming together and makes sense? Paul says, "Here's the reason we are acceptable to GOD. When we chose to follow CHRIST, HIS blood covered our sins. When GOD sees us, HE doesn't see the nature of our sins. HE sees the power of HIS Son's blood. And, what can wash away my sins? Nothing but the blood of JESUS.

According to verse 29, because the price that CHRIST paid on the cross, it connected us to HIS Son. We are connected to HIS Son through CHRIST's blood. JESUS connects us to GOD. Which makes us one big happy family; all connected in the Spirit. When you are connected, you have been approved. Verse 31, *What can we say about all of this? If GOD is for us, who can be against us?* In other words, GOD says, "I got you. You just need to know that I got you."

To back-up everything Paul just said in verses 29 – 30, look at verses 32 – 34. *GOD didn't spare HIS own Son but handed Him over to death for all of us. So HE will also give us everything along with Him. Who will accuse those whom GOD has chosen? GOD has approved of them. Who will condemn them? CHRIST has died, and more importantly, He was brought back to life. CHRIST has the highest position in heaven. CHRIST also intercedes for us.* Not only do we have the HOLY SPIRIT interceding and making intercession on our behalf, verse 34 says, CHRIST also intercedes for us. Everybody say, no excuse!

It's not to say we don't have an excuse to sin, which we never have an excuse to sin. But, what this implies is, that when we fall we don't have an excuse not to get back up. We don't have an excuse not to *continue in well-doing*. We don't have an excuse to practice sin. We have every reason to get back up and follow GOD's plan. No excuses!

Verses 35 – 37 alleviate all the excuses. *What will separate us from the love CHRIST has for us? Can trouble, distress, persecution, hunger, nakedness, danger, or violent death separate us from His love? As Scripture says: "We are being killed all day long because of you. We are thought of as sheep to be slaughtered."* But, *The one who loves us gives us an overwhelming victory in all these difficulties.*

Because we are connected to CHRIST in verse 35, verse 36 says the enemy is going to try to do everything he can to separate us. That's why our corrupt nature is going to always be at war with our Spiritual nature. Our corrupt nature is going to always try to influence our flesh with sin. The enemy knows if he can get us to practice sin, to live a lifestyle of sin, it will separate us from GOD. That's why I said earlier, that the enemy wants us to feel that GOD is no longer with us. He knows it will cause us to continue in our sin and will hinder us from continuing in *well-doing*.

Paul closes out chapter 8 with verses 38 and 39. *I am convinced that nothing can ever separate us from GOD's love which CHRIST JESUS our Lord shows us. We can't be separated by death or life, by angels or rulers, by anything in the present or anything in the future, by forces or powers in the world above or in the world below, or by anything else in creation.* Falling short doesn't separate us from GOD. Living a lifestyle of sin does. For us to *continue in well-doing*, the HOLY SPIRIT grieves, intercedes, and makes intercessions on our behalf. If you don't believe that practicing sin and living a lifestyle of sin separates you from GOD, then go back to Romans 1:28. *And even as they did not like to retain GOD in their knowledge, GOD gave them over to a reprobate mind, to do those things which are not fitting.*

Verses 38 and 39 assure us that there is no power, no ruler, and no demonic force that can snatch us away from GOD. The only thing that can separate us from GOD is our willingness to live a lifestyle of sin. GOD says, before I allow sin to separate us, I'm going to fight like heaven by grieving, interceding, and making intercessions on your behalf.

Chapter 9
Paul's Concerns

Paul's Concern for the Jewish People
Verses 1-23

Chapter 9 is a lot different than the other chapters that we have already covered. As a matter of fact, in all the other chapters, Paul has been talking to us about our liberty from The Law. He teaches us how no sin has control over us, we have control over it. After grace has done its job, GOD adopts us into HIS family. Which now makes us the children of GOD. HE is our FATHER, and we are HIS children.

In this chapter, Paul goes further into detail about our adoption, because the Jews felt that they did not need adopting. They felt they were born into GOD's family by race and not by faith. That's why Paul constantly uses the word adoption. To be adopted, in this sense, means you have to be chosen. You can't inherit GOD. HE first has to examine your faith and then HE chooses you to be HIS child.

The privilege of being adopted is, that adoption shows how much GOD loves us. Not only does it shows how much HE loves us, but it also shows just how much HE wants us. Think about it, pregnancies can be unwanted. Couples adopt children, because they want them. They choose the children they want, even though they know that child is going to grow up and make mistakes. They adopt them anyway.

That's why GOD adopts us. HE knows we're going to mess up and going to fall short. However, HE adopts us, because HE wants and loves us, and because HE loves us. HE chooses us. There's no such thing as an unwanted adoption in The Kingdom.

That's the conversation that Paul is having with the Jews in chapter 9. A lot of the Jews felt they inherited GOD. They believed they inherited the relationship with GOD which prevented them from establishing a relationship with HIM. A lot of them were Jews by race and not by faith. Your race doesn't guarantee you GOD's promises, your faith does. The Jews thought just because of their race, they inherited GOD's promises, regardless of their faith.

Verses 1-4 Paul says *As a Christian, I'm telling you the truth. I'm not lying. The HOLY SPIRIT, along with my own thoughts, supports me in this. I have deep sorrow and endless heartache. I wish I could be condemned and cut off from CHRIST for the sake of others who, like me, are Jewish by birth. They are Israelites, GOD's adopted children. They have the Lord's glory, the pledges, Moses' Teachings, the true worship, and the promises.*

The Jews had a major problem. They couldn't embrace the idea that GOD had established a faith of people and not a race of people. A lot of them had a problem, because Paul was offering a relationship with GOD to everybody, and he was bringing people into the faith. The Jews became offended, because the people Paul brought into the faith weren't a part of their race.

The Jews turned from their faith and made it all about race. Their outlook on being part of GOD's children is that it was not about being born into the faith, but being of the Jewish race. They did not like the fact that if it was all about the faith, then anybody that believed could be a part of the family. When the Jews made it all about race, no one outside of their race could have a relationship with GOD. That's why they felt their race were the only people entitled to GOD, and the only ones entitled to the promises of GOD, even if they didn't have faith in GOD.

How can you have a relationship with GOD and belong to GOD and not have faith in the GOD you have a relationship with? They denied CHRIST, even though He was of the same race and the same faith. If they had held onto their faith, it would have been easier to accept CHRIST as their Savior. Because a lot of Jews think they are acceptable to GOD by race, a lot of them never become saved. A lot of so-called "religious folks" never receive salvation, because they think they inherited GOD's acceptance.

Verse 5, *The Messiah is descended from their ancestors according to His human nature.* Race! *The Messiah is GOD over everything, forever blessed. Amen.* Faith! That's why it was so easy for them to worship idol gods. They were more focused on their race and not their faith. Paul is trying to explain to them, that you don't belong to GOD because of your race. You belong to HIM according to your faith.

In verses 6-8, *Now it is not as though GOD's word has failed. Clearly, not everyone descended from Israel is part of Israel or a descendant of Abraham. However, as Scripture says, "Through Isaac, your descendants will carry on your name." This means that children born by natural descent from Abraham are not necessarily GOD's children. Instead, children born by the promise are considered Abraham's descendants.*

GOD established HIS covenant and promises through Abraham. The only reason HE established HIS covenant with Abraham is because of Abraham's faith. Abraham's faith established the covenant. The covenant attaches Abraham to GOD's promises. For Abraham's seed, his children and his offspring to receive the same promises, they first had to have Abraham's faith which attached them to the covenant which gave them the promises.

The problem with the Jews was that they thought that just because they were born under the lineage of Abraham, it automatically attached them to GOD's covenant which gave them GOD's promises. Paul tells them that just because they were born in the race of Abraham doesn't mean that they would inherit the faith of Abraham.

To be a child of GOD, you have to come by faith, not by race. Paul says, "You can't be born into GOD's family. GOD has to adopt you into HIS family according to your faith." That's what grace does. It examines our faith and sees if it is like Abraham's faith. Once our faith is like Abraham's faith, grace takes CHRIST's sacrifice and covers us in His blood. This then makes us acceptable to GOD. Once we become acceptable to GOD, according to our faith, GOD adopts us into HIS family making us HIS children. Since we are HIS adopted children, we are now heirs to HIS promises. It's that simple!

Before we go any further, I want to pause and ask this question. Do you believe the church makes this same mistake today and how? I, personally, don't think we reject people based on their race. I believe we reject people because of their denomination. A lot of denominations feel that they're the only ones going to heaven. They do not realize GOD never established a denomination of people. HE established a faith of people. As long as we are all a part of that same faith, the same faith of Abraham, then GOD accepts us as HIS child.

Paul says to the Jews, "How dare you think you are entitled to GOD's promises just because of your race." This is heartbreaking to GOD. How can you be a part of the race and not be willing to embrace the faith? For example, GOD makes me a promise that HE's going to bless me. The blessing is going to affect my children, their children, their children, and their children. The promises don't just pass on to them. They first have to agree that they want the promises before they can receive them. When it comes time to receive the promises, if they have not agreed that they want them, they don't just get them because they are my children. Why? They have not agreed that they want them. If they refuse to receive them, then my attitude is, let me adopt some children that will. GOD decides how HE wants HIS promises distributed.

When it comes to GOD's acceptance, it's all about our faith. HE accepts us according to our faith. Not only does HE accepts us according to our faith, but HE also blesses us according to our faith. If GOD blesses us according to our faith, it doesn't do me any good to get upset about what

GOD is doing for someone else. I may not trust GOD on the same level as they do. I think that's a major problem in the Church. A lot of people look at what GOD is doing for someone else, and because GOD is not doing that for them, they tend to have a problem with that person. That person may trust GOD on a greater level. They see the glory, but don't know the story.

The Jews thought that as long as they were born into the family of faith and follow The Law, they were entitled to the promises. The problem was, that they hadn't agreed that they wanted the promises. They just felt entitled to them. It's the same way in the church today. A lot of people think that just because they are a member of the church, or grew up in church, automatically makes them a Christian. Everybody in the church is not a part of the family. That's the danger with religions and denominations; people end up establishing a relationship with their religion and not GOD.

Verses 9-12, *For example, this is what the promise said, "I will come back at the right time, and Sarah will have a son." The same thing happened to Rebekah. Rebekah became pregnant by our ancestor Isaac. Before the children had been born or had done anything good or bad, Rebekah was told that the older child would serve the younger one. This was said to Rebekah so that GOD's plan would remain a matter of his choice, a choice based on GOD's call and not on anything people do.*

Paul said GOD has established the way HE wants to distribute HIS promises. The reason HE established HIS family that way is so anybody can't be born into it. Remember in Matthew when JESUS was talking about the Kingdom of GOD? A young man walked up to JESUS and said, "How can I inherit eternal life? I have been doing everything the Law requires." (Matthew 19:16-20) JESUS says to him in verse 21, "Yes, you have established a relationship with the Law and with your stuff. You haven't established a relationship with Me. Sale all your stuff, and come follow Me." When you feel like you can inherit the Kingdom, you will never try to receive salvation for yourself. It will cause you to live any way you choose without feeling rejected.

Verse 13, *The Scriptures say, "I loved Jacob, but I hated Esau."* GOD said, "Your law tried to dictate who can receive MY promises. Your law says it should be passed to the oldest. The Law doesn't choose who receives MY promises. I do! MY promises are distributed by faith; not by race."

Verses 14-16, *What can we say? That GOD is unfair? That's unthinkable! For example, GOD said to Moses, "I will be kind to anyone I want to. I will be merciful to anyone I want to." Therefore, GOD's choice does not depend on a person's desire or effort, but on GOD's mercy.*

Who are we to try and dictate who can and who cannot receive GOD's blessing? That's just like someone saying, "The only way you can receive this healing is if you sow a certain amount." I'm sorry, when did GOD give us the authority on deciding who can and who cannot receive HIS healing and blessings? According to the text, GOD said to Moses, I can bless whoever I want to.

If you're telling me I can only receive blessings if I sow an offering, then that blessing wasn't from GOD. That's what you call witchcraft. Money doesn't move GOD, faith does! Why would I pay someone for a 'witchcraft blessing' when I can just trust GOD and have faith and receive a miracle? The world's promises are temporary. GOD's promises are eternal. (2nd Corinthians 4:18)

I believe in sowing according to my faith. Not because GOD has given someone authority over HIS blessings. The moment someone takes ownership of what belongs to GOD, it becomes witchcraft. I don't want that type of blessing. Anything you take that belongs to GOD becomes cursed.

In verse 17, GOD doesn't make it any simpler than this. *For example, Scripture says to Pharaoh, "I put you here for this reason: to demonstrate my power; through you. Not take ownership of it. I put you here to spread MY name throughout the earth.* GOD says, "I bless you so MY name can be great." If someone is charging people for HIS blessings, the only one that's getting all the glory is the individual. GOD says, "I didn't bless you so your name can be great. I bless you so MINE can be great."

Verses 18-19, *Therefore, if GOD wants to be kind to anyone, HE will be. If HE wants to make someone stubborn, HE will. You may ask me, "Why does GOD still find fault with anyone? Who can resist whatever GOD wants to do?"* That's like saying, "Yes, GOD I want to be blessed with YOUR blessings. But, I want YOUR blessings under my conditions." Paul says, "Who does that?" GOD is sovereign. How can we the creation have the audacity to question the CREATOR about something HE created? How dare we question GOD about something that belongs to HIM?

Verse 20, *Who do you think you are to talk back to GOD like that? Can an object that was made say to its maker, "Why did you make me like this?"* However GOD made me, I'm going to always appreciate what HE made. How dare I alter something GOD made? Verse 21, *A potter has the right to do whatever he wants with his clay. He can make something for a special occasion or something for everyday use from the same lump of clay.*

Why would I have a problem with how GOD made you when the same POTTER that made you also made me? If we are made from the same lump of clay, I just need to figure out why HE made me. If a potter decided to take a lump of clay and create a plate and a bowl, the bowl can't look down on the plate because it was made differently. Even though they have different uses, they both were made from the same clay.

The problem in society is, that too many people are trying to make themselves resemble something that GOD didn't make. Paul says, how can the clay question the potter about what the potter made? Everyone GOD made HE perfectly made them. If we are made from the same lump of clay, instead of me getting mad because of what GOD is doing for someone else, all I have to do is increase my faith in GOD and watch HIM turn around and do it for me. Romans 2:11 says *For there is no respect of persons with GOD.*

My attitude has always been, that President Obama is not better than me because he is the first black President. The same GOD that made him also made me. HE made us from the same lump of clay. When GOD made him, HE made him to be the president. When GOD made me, HE made me to preach and teach HIS word. How can one lump be better than the other lump when we both were made from the same lump? I'm just glad that HE created my lump into something and didn't throw my lump away.

Remember, how the Jews use to think they were better than everyone else? They thought they were better, so they looked down on everyone else. Not realizing that the people they were looking down at were made from the same clay they were made from. Paul deals with this situation in the next two verses.

Verses 22 – 23, *If GOD wants to demonstrate HIS anger and reveal HIS power, HE can do it. But can't HE be extremely patient with people who are objects of HIS anger because they are headed for destruction? Can't GOD also reveal the riches of HIS glory to people who are objects of HIS mercy and who HE had already prepared for glory?* This is a message the Church needs to hear. Paul says in verse 22, why can't GOD be patient with those who are headed for destruction? How soon do we forget? We in The Body of CHRIST are so quick to offer wrath and destruction to other people. The same GOD that saved us is trying to save them also. Paul said, "GOD can show them mercy just like HE stepped in and showed us mercy."

Just like GOD is patient with those who are headed for destruction, Paul says in verse 23, that HE can also bless those who have already received mercy how HE chooses to. Paul said all this to simply say this, this is GOD's show! We don't have the right to question how HE decides to run HIS show.

GOD Chose People Who Are Not Jewish
Verses 24-33

Verses 24-29, *Even us, whom he hath called, not of the Jews only, but also of the Gentiles? As he saith also in Osee, I will call them my people, which were not my people; and her beloved, which was not beloved. And it shall come to pass, that in the place where it was said unto them, Ye are not my people; there shall they be called the children of the living GOD. Esaias also crieth concerning Israel, Though the number of the children of Israel be as the sand of the sea, a remnant shall be saved: For he will finish the work, and cut it short in righteousness: because a short work will the Lord make upon the earth. And as Esaias said before, Except the Lord of Sabaoth had left us a seed, we had been as Sodoma, and been made like unto Gomorrha. So what can we say? We can say that those who were not Jews, who were not trying to gain GOD's approval won HIS approval, an approval based on their faith.*

How did they receive GOD's righteousness? How did they receive GOD's mercy? Not by their race, their works, their denomination nor their religion. Only by their faith! The main ones that thought they inherited GOD's righteousness, were the same ones that thought they owned GOD's mercy and had a monopoly on GOD. Look at what Paul tells them in verse 31. *The people of Israel tried to gain GOD's approval by obeying Moses' Teachings, but they did not reach their goal.*

Do you know how many people in the church are trying to tell other people they can't receive salvation and don't have it themselves? How many people in the church are missing GOD, because they think they already have HIM? They think they have salvation, but never have been saved because they missed GOD?

The same ones that are trying to make others jump through hoops to get GOD's approval don't have it themselves. You can't deny me something that not only doesn't belong to you, but you don't even have. Paul said the people of Israel, the Jews, tried to gain GOD's approval by obeying their laws. They thought they had GOD because their focus was on their race, their laws, their bylaws and their denomination. But, they missed GOD.

Here's how they missed GOD.

Verses 32-33, *Why? They didn't rely on faith to gain GOD's approval, but they relied on their own efforts. They stumbled over the rock that trips people. As Scripture says, "I am placing a rock in Zion that people trip over, a large rock that people find offensive. Whoever believes in him will not be ashamed."* A lot of people are going to miss GOD stumbling over their religion, denomination and/or their title.

Chapter 10

Just Believe

If You Believe, You Will Be Saved
Verses 1-21

Being Jewish was never supposed to be about race. When GOD established HIS people, it was all about faith. Verse 1, *Brothers and sisters, my heart's desire and prayer to GOD on behalf of the Jewish people is that they would be saved.* Who was Paul wishing would get saved? The Jews. But hold up, these are GOD's chosen people. These are the ones from Abraham's lineage. Somewhere between Abraham's faith, they made it all about race and not about faith, because they didn't have faith.

Look at what Paul says in verse 1. I wish they were saved. One of the most hurtful things in the Body of CHRIST is to see someone who thinks they are saved because of what they practice and not because of what they believe. Remember what Paul told us before, "We know what you believe by how you choose to live." Someone can easily live a lifestyle of sin, thinking they're on their way to heaven, and since they think they're on their way to heaven, it causes them not to seek deliverance from their sins.

The sad reality is, you can say you believe one way, but live your lifestyle opposite of what you say you believe. GOD doesn't allow sinners into heaven. HE only allows those who have been delivered from their sins and have been made the righteousness of GOD. That's why JESUS said that when He comes back, HE's looking for Believers without spot or wrinkle. (Ephesians 5:27) Not those who are perfect, but those whose grace has been covered with JESUS's blood. How can grace cover your sins when you refuse to stop practicing sins?

Verses 2, *I can assure you that they are deeply devoted to GOD, but they are misguided.* Paul says, they have a zeal for GOD, that's why they're here. They want GOD on their terms and not HIS. Verse 3, *They don't understand how to receive GOD's approval. So, they try to set up their way to get it, and they have not accepted GOD's way for receiving HIS approval.*

They think they can be a practicing sinner and still go to heaven, because they have established their way to get to heaven. In verse 4 Paul says, "You can't get GOD's approval on your terms. The only way HE will accept you is on HIS terms." *CHRIST is the fulfillment of Moses' Teachings so that everyone who has faith may receive GOD's approval.* If you don't go through CHRIST, you don't get GOD's approval. That's why the moment you say you believe, grace steps in and examines your confession and sees if your confession is real or not. The reason grace has to step in and examine our confession is because of what verse 2 says. They have a zeal for GOD. However, they are not ready to change.

Many people join the church and think they are saved just because they have a zeal or a passion for GOD. When you're not ready to change, you function as verse 3 states and establish your own righteousness and refused to submit to the righteousness of GOD. So, grace steps in and says, "I'm sorry I can't cover you because you're not ready to change. It doesn't do me any good to cover your sins with JESUS' blood and you continue to practice living in sin. Why would I give you the authority over sin and you choose to still be in bondage to sin? So, when you are ready to stop being a slave to sin, then I will cover you with JESUS' blood."

The same individuals who have a zeal for GOD, and practice religion and tradition think they are saved. Your zeal doesn't save you. Your faith does. Verse 4, *For CHRIST is the end of the law for righteousness to everyone who believes.* If your righteousness does not line up with CHRIST's righteousness, then you're not approved. What is the opposite of approved?

Rejected. It's almost as if, on the last day, everyone is going to have a sign that says either approved or rejected.

Matthew 7:21-24, *JESUS says Not every one that saith unto me, Lord, Lord, shall enter into the kingdom of heaven; but he that doeth the will of my Father which is in heaven. Many will say to me in that day, Lord, Lord, have we not prophesied in thy name? and in thy name have cast out devils? and in thy name done many wonderful works? And then will I profess unto them, I never knew you: depart from me, ye that work iniquity.*

Here's how you will know who belongs to GOD. Matthew 7:24 says *Therefore, everyone who hears what I say and obeys...* Not those who establish their own righteousness. We must hear HIS sayings and also do them. JESUS says, *it will be like a wise person who built a house on rock.* Basically, no one can sneak their way into heaven. You can't sing, preach or work your way into heaven. You have to live your way into heaven.

I don't know why people think living for GOD is so hard. GOD says, "I don't expect for you to be perfect. I expect you to fall short. If you're going to represent ME and live by faith, I expect you to at least strive to live right. If you fall, I don't expect you to continue in your sin." What does HE expect us to do? To *continue in well-doing*. Why does HE expect us to *continue* in *well-doing*? HE has given us authority and power over sin. We are no longer in bondage to sin, but we have dominion over it.

Watch how Paul explains the misconception in verses 5 and 6. *Moses writes about receiving GOD's approval by following the Mosaic laws. Moses said, "The person who obeys the laws will live because of the laws he obeys." However, Scripture talks about GOD's approval which is based on their faith...* Here's the big misconception. Paul said most people think that since they are religious and they follow religious practices, that makes them acceptable to GOD. Scripture says, what makes you acceptable to GOD is what you believe. Our practices don't save us, our faith does!

After Paul says we receive GOD's approval *based on our faith*, he continues to say in verse 6 *"Don't ask yourself who will go up to heaven," (that is, to bring CHRIST down).* Verse 7 says *"Don't ask who will go down into the depths," (that is, to bring CHRIST back from the dead).* Now, to understand verses 6 and 7, you have to go back to the verse before 6, which is verse 5, and the verse after 7, which is verse 8.

In verse 5, the Jews thought one received salvation by keeping Moses' Laws. In verse 8, Paul talks about the message we declare to receive salvation. In other words, here's how you receive salvation. To ask the question in verse 6 *who will go up to heaven* and then ask the question in verse 7 *who will go down into the depths* is an insult to the work that CHRIST has already done. To ask those questions is to suggest that salvation comes by our own efforts and not by our faith. That's why I said before, the practice of your tradition can't get you into heaven. You have to believe and live your way into heaven.

By CHRIST dying and then resurrecting, the fullness of salvation was made possible. HE doesn't have to die again. Neither does HE have to resurrect again. The mere fact that HE died and was resurrected the first time, means we don't have to bring HIM down nor bring HIM back from the dead. The work was already done the first time. To suggest there's any other way to receive salvation is an insult to the work HE has already done the first time.

Verse 8, *However, what else does it say? "This message is near you. It's in your mouth and in your heart." This is the message of faith that we spread.* The key to unlocking salvation's door is found in your heart and mouth. That's why grace has to examine our confession to see what's in our mouths is also what we say we believe in our hearts.

The danger is when people have a zeal for something. The zeal causes all kinds of stuff to come out of their mouths. That's why Paul said in verse 2 they have a zeal for GOD, but they are blinded by their own self-righteousness. When you have a zeal for GOD and have established your own righteousness, then you want GOD, but you want HIM on your terms and not HIS. GOD doesn't approve us based on our terms. HE approves us based on HIS terms. Remember verse 4? *CHRIST is the fulfillment of Moses' Teachings so that everyone who has faith may receive GOD's approval.*

Verse 8 the message of faith *is in your mouth and in your heart.* In verse 9, Paul tells them the message that is supposed to be in their heart and mouths is the confession of faith. *If you declare that JESUS is Lord, and believe that GOD brought Him back to life, you will be saved.* The message of faith that should be in our hearts and mouths is that JESUS is Lord and GOD raised JESUS from the dead.

Paul then describes the importance of this message in our hearts and our mouth in verse 10. In other words, here's why this message unlocks the door to salvation. *For with the heart one believes unto righteousness, and with the mouth, confession is made unto salvation.* Paul just backed up everything he's been saying. Look at verse 10 again. *For with the heart one believes unto righteousness.* In the corridors of my salvation, I believe in my heart that I'm supposed to live right; according to GOD's righteousness. You will know what I believe based on how I live and not based on what just comes out of my mouth.

What's in my heart shows up in my lifestyle and how I choose to live. Because, with the heart, we believe unto righteousness and not our own self-righteousness, but the righteousness of CHRIST. My lifestyle should be the evidence that I'm striving to live right. Why? That's what's in my heart. I can't live outside of GOD's righteousness if I believe in HIS righteousness in my heart.

I believe people who have a passion for GOD in their heart, but are not willing to live for GOD through their lifestyle don't believe in their heart unto righteousness. That's why Paul makes it simple to determine who is saved. If their lifestyle doesn't line up with their confession, according to the confession of faith, you can't be saved.

That's why Paul says in verse 3, *For they being ignorant of GOD's righteousness, and seeking to establish their own righteousness, have not submitted to the righteousness of GOD.* You can't receive salvation with your confession and your own righteousness. You only receive salvation by confessing that you are willing to accept GOD's righteousness. That's why Paul tells us in verse 9 we're supposed to confess with our mouth the Lord JESUS.

If you are choosing to live by your own righteousness and not GOD's righteousness, your confession should be, "I confess to myself." If I have established my righteousness, then with my heart I don't believe unto HIS righteousness. You can't receive salvation with your confession and your own righteousness. You only receive salvation by confessing that you are willing to accept GOD's righteousness. That's why grace has to examine our hearts and see if our confession is based on GOD's righteousness and not our own.

When our heart believes unto HIS righteousness, look at what your confession does: confession is made unto salvation. Your confession then opens the door to salvation. That's why it is easy to tell who is truly saved. If their lifestyle does not line up with their confession of what they say they believe, then my question is, how was grace able to save them? I don't care what someone practices or how long they've been in church. What you believe can't just be in your mouth. It has to also be in your heart. The mouth has to confess what is in the heart.

Verse 11, Scripture says, *"Whoever believes in Him will not be ashamed."* If the confession of faith is what I truly believe in my heart, I should not be ashamed to confess what's in my heart out of my mouth. It should never be a problem with us declaring what we believe in our hearts.

If I think I can become saved just because of what's in my heart, but I'm ashamed to confess it out of my mouth, then I don't unlock the door to salvation. Verse 10 (KJV) said *with the mouth confession is made unto salvation.* There are many people who will say, "Well, that's what I believe." But, have you confessed it? Grace wants to match your confession to what you believe in your heart. If I'm ashamed to stand before man and confess what I believe in my heart, how can I be bold enough to stand before GOD?

The reason confession is so important is because the moment we become a Believer, we are charged to go and be a witness. How can someone be a witness if they are afraid to confess what they believe? Could you imagine how powerful our testimony is to someone who has received the message of faith? If you confess what you believe in your heart, not only will they hear what you believe coming out of your mouth, but they can see what you believe by how you choose to live.

When I share with people what I believe, I don't just want them to hear it. I want them to be a witness to it. I want them to see what I believe. I want them to see that what I believe works. That's why I confess what I believe so passionately. I choose to live by what I believe.

Verse 12, *There is no difference between Jews and Greeks. They all have the same Lord, who gives HIS riches to everyone who calls on HIM.* When Paul says, *There is no difference between Jews and Greeks*, what Paul did was so profound. You would think he was saying there's no difference between the races. Look at the terms Paul used. He used Jews; faith! Greeks; race! Let me explain. Remember Jews were not a race. It was faith. Greeks are a race of people. Evidently, the audience he was talking to thought they belonged to GOD because of their race and not by their faith. Again, being a Jew was not their race. It was supposed to be their faith.

Paul compared what they thought was their race, and says GOD accepts us based on our faith. And because every Believer shares the same faith, we all have the same Lord. Since we share the same Lord, we belong to the same family regardless of our race, but based on our faith. Even when JESUS came, He was trying to explain to the Jews, "You are not supposed to be a race of people. You are supposed to be a faith of people."

Verse 13, *So then, "Whosoever calls on the name of the Lord will be saved."* Did you identify the keyword in verse 13? *Whosoever*. Paul says it was never about race because *whosoever*. Our race doesn't make us family, our faith does. Anybody who trusts GOD and is not ashamed to confess HIS Son JESUS as Lord shall be saved.

Verse 14, *But how can people call on Him if they have not believed in Him? How can they believe in Him if they have not heard His message? How can they hear if no one tells the Good News to them?* This message of faith has to be heard for someone to accept it. If they don't hear it, how can they accept it?

If you are a Believer and you run across an unbeliever, how can you expect them to accept CHRIST if you are ashamed to share what you believe? If we refuse to share what we believe with those who don't believe, then we adopt the same attitude the Jews had. We think CHRIST only belongs to us when HE died for the world. The world needs to know HE died for them also. The only way the world will ever hear this message is that the Believers have to share the message.

Verse 15, *How can people tell the Good News if no one sends them? As Scripture says, "How beautiful are the feet of the messengers who announce the Good News."* Here's the mistake The Church makes. For some reason, we only think verse 15 applies to Pastors. And because we think it only refers to Pastors, then Believers become lazy with sharing the message of CHRIST. Verse 15 refers to anybody who spreads the Good News about JESUS. Anytime you share the message of faith, not only are you witnessing, but you're also proclaiming, announcing, and broadcasting the message of faith.

All Believers are called to spread the Good News of CHRIST. Not all Believers are called to Pastor GOD's people. Just because someone shares the message of JESUS CHRIST, does not mean they were called to Pastor and lead. We are all called to witness the message of faith.

When GOD calls someone to Pastor, HE calls them to tend to HIS Sheep/Believers. HE calls us to equip the Believers so they can go out and spread the message. Once the Believers are equipped with the message, they are sent out and required to go make disciples.

Verses 16 and 17, *But they have not all obeyed the Gospel. For Isaiah says, "Lord, who has believed our message?" So then faith comes by hearing and hearing by the word of GOD.* Every time you hear the Word of GOD and receive understanding, it should increase your faith. Not only should it increase your faith, but every time you hear it and receive understanding, you're supposed to go out and share the message you heard. Verse 14 says, "How will people ever hear the message if you never share the message you heard." This message of faith has to be heard for someone to accept it. If they don't hear it, how can they accept it? If faith comes by hearing the Word of GOD, the moment we hear it and understand it, we are required to share it by witnessing it. Now, can I get a "witness"?

In verse 18, while Paul is writing this letter, he's asking himself a rhetorical question. "Well, if it's that easy, did not Israel get the message? Why are they constantly rejecting the message of faith if it comes from hearing? Why are they lacking in the faith department if they are constantly hearing the Word of GOD?" Look at verse 18, *But I ask, "Didn't they hear that message?" Certainly, they did! "The voice of the messengers has gone out into the whole world and their words to the ends of the earth."*

To answer his question, look at what Paul says in the remaining verses 19 through 21. *Again I ask, "Didn't Israel understand that message?" Moses was the first to say, "I will make you jealous of people who are not a nation. I will make you angry about a nation that doesn't understand." Isaiah said very boldly, "I was found by those who weren't looking for me. I was revealed to those who weren't asking for me."* Then Isaiah said about Israel, *"All day long I have stretched out my hands to disobedient and rebellious people."*

Some people reject the message of faith, because they are rebellious people. Others hear the message, understand the message, and then turn around and reject the message, because they are just disobedient people. While sharing the Gospel, some people just won't receive it. As Believers, we're not responsible for following them home and making sure they obey it. That's why we are called witnesses and not spiritual enforcers. It's our job to spread the message of JESUS. It's their job to accept and believe the message of JESUS.

Can I mess some of you up? Some people hear the message of faith and believe the message. But, because of their rebellious spirit, they refuse to confess the message they believe. If every Believer spreads the message of faith to everyone they come in contact with, at least on judgment day, they won't be able to say they never heard it. It's our job to spread it. It's their job to accept it. It's not our job as Believers to make people believe or confess; to accept or reject. It's our job to make sure the message is heard. They may reject the message after hearing it, but their excuse should never be they never heard it. Now go and be a witness!

Chapter 11
GOD's Continous Love

When we enter into chapter 11, Paul asked a very important question in verse 1. Remember the question Paul asked in chapter 10. The question still remains since *faith comes by hearing and hearing by the word of GOD*, then why do the Jews not have faith? They heard the Word of GOD all the time, yet they don't have faith. The reason they didn't have faith is that they would rather embrace their race instead of faith.

Paul's important question in chapter 11 verse 1 is, *So, I ask, "Has GOD rejected HIS people Israel?" Of course not; that's unheard of!* GOD will never reject those that belong to HIM by faith. We belong to GOD because of our faith, not because of our zeal, tradition, nor because of our denomination. It is only by what we choose to believe in our hearts. What we believe in our hearts, should show up in our lifestyle.

Look at what Paul continues to say in verse 1. *Consider this. I'm an Israelite myself, a descendant of Abraham from the tribe of Benjamin.* Verses 2-6, GOD has not rejected HIS people, but HIS people have rejected HIM by faith. Paul says, and to prove to you that GOD established a faith of people and not a race of people, look at what Paul continues to say. *Don't you know what Elijah says in the Scripture passage when he complained to GOD about Israel? He said, "LORD, they've killed your prophets and torn down your altars. I'm the only one left, and they're trying to take my life." But what was GOD's reply? GOD said, "I've kept 7,000 people for MYSELF who have not knelt to worship Baal." So, as there were then, there are now a few left that GOD has chosen by HIS kindness. If they were chosen by GOD's kindness, they weren't chosen because of anything they did. Otherwise, GOD's kindness wouldn't be kindness.*

Out of all the millions of so-called Jews, GOD said, I kept 7,000 of them to MYSELF. GOD said, "The reason I kept them for ME is not because of their race, but because of their faith. Those 7,000 who refused to bow down to Baal belong to ME by faith."

The reason Paul is going back and forth regarding this same question is that he knew some people wouldn't grasp the idea that being a Jew wasn't about race, but it was about faith. He understood that some people wouldn't grasp the idea that GOD accepts us based on our faith. If you believe in your heart, HE accepts you. If you don't believe in your heart, HE rejects you. For some reason, they couldn't understand that if GOD rejects them, how can HE reject HIS people?

Paul kept trying to explain to them that GOD doesn't reject those who believe by faith. Those who believe by faith belong to HIM. Those that don't believe, don't. It's just that simple!

It's the same concept we have today. We think just because someone is in church, that automatically makes them saved. You're not saved because you're in church, you're saved because of what you believe and how you choose to live. You can look like a Believer all day long. If you don't live like a Believer then you're not one. You can shout, dance, and jump up and down. If what's in your heart doesn't match the confession that comes out of your mouth, then you're just shouting and dancing. You have a zeal for GOD, but it's not because you belong to GOD.

Verse 7, *So, what does all this mean? It means that Israel has never achieved what it has been striving for. However, those whom God has chosen have achieved it. The minds of the rest of Israel were closed,...* Paul says, It simply means that Israel has never achieved what it has been striving for. However, those who GOD has elected, chosen by faith, have obtained it, and the rest of them didn't. Do you know how many people in the church think they have obtained salvation just because they are in church? This is hurtful to GOD. A lot of people think that just because they are in church, they have obtained it. Obtained what? Salvation. You can always tell who doesn't have it based on the lifestyle they choose to live.

Look at verses 8 – 10, *as Scripture says, "To this day GOD has given them a spirit of deep sleep. Their eyes don't see, and their ears don't hear!" And David says, "Let the table set for them become a trap and a net, a snare and a punishment for them. Let their vision become clouded so that they cannot see. Let them carry back-breaking burdens forever."*

The reason it was so hurtful to GOD was that a lot of the Jews were from Abraham's lineage. If anybody should have kept the faith, Abraham's family should have. They thought they belong to GOD because they were in Abraham's lineage. It's hard to get someone to embrace the faith when they think they already have it.

Could you imagine trying to get a Pastor, who preaches The Gospel every Sunday, that they need salvation? Or someone who has grown up in the church their whole life that they're not saved? When you look at their lifestyle, it's evident that they're not saved, because of how they choose to live. Notice I said, choose to live and not struggle to live.

How are you going to know the Word and not be saved by the Word you know? Every Pastor who thinks it's okay to live as a sinner just because you're in love with someone regardless of their gender, needs to be saved. Every so-called Believer that thinks living a lifestyle of any sin is okay needs saving. I'm not talking about falling short, I'm talking about living a lifestyle of sin.

1st Corinthians 6:9-11, *Do you not know that the unrighteous will not inherit the Kingdom of GOD? Do not be deceived. Neither fornicators, nor idolaters, nor adulterers, nor homosexuals, nor sodomites, nor thieves, nor covetous, nor drunkards, nor revilers, nor extortioners will inherit the Kingdom of GOD.* The reason I chose to insert 1st Corinthians 6:9-11 is so you'll know what the Bible says instead of what my opinion is.

To prove that those who have been delivered from sin are no longer labeled by their sins, look at what verse 11 says. *And such were some of you. But you were washed, but you were sanctified, but you were justified in the name of the Lord JESUS and by the SPIRIT of our GOD.* The moment we become saved, we are no longer labeled by our sins. You're only labeled by sin when you live a life of that sin, because then it's a practice. I wouldn't be considered a dentist just because I pulled someone's tooth out. I would only be considered a dentist if that was my practice.

Paul has been teaching us that if you have truly been saved by grace, how can you practice and live a life of any sin? Unless, you just have a zeal for GOD, but refuse to live for GOD. It is possible to have a zeal and a passion for GOD and still walk in sin. Once again, we're not saved by our zeal. We are saved because *with the heart man believes unto righteousness.* (Romans 10:10)

Verses 11-12, *So I ask, "Has Israel stumbled so badly that it can't get up again?" That's unthinkable! By Israel's failure, salvation has come to people who are not Jewish to make the Jewish people jealous. The fall of the Jewish people made the world spiritually rich. Their failure made people who are not Jewish spiritually rich. So the inclusion of Jewish people will make the world even richer.*

Paul says 'Since y'all want to talk about race, even though GOD established a faith, if anybody should have kept the faith, it should have been those in the lineage of Abraham. Why? The promise was given to Abraham and his seeds. Instead of y'all keeping the faith, y'all neglected the faith and turned it into a race. Salvation is available to anyone who chooses to believe outside of Abraham's seed." That's worth a shout!

Watch how Paul so eloquently explains this in verses 13 – 15. *Now, I speak to you who are not Jewish. As long as I am an apostle sent to people who are not Jewish, I bring honor to my ministry. Perhaps I can make my people jealous and save some of them. If Israel's rejection means that the world has been brought back to GOD, what does Israel's acceptance mean? It means that Israel has come back to life.*

When the promise was given to Abraham and his seeds, the overall plan was to reconcile the world back to GOD through the promise made to Abraham and his seeds. The Jews thought GOD was only coming back for their race. What they didn't realize was that GOD was trying to reconcile the world through our faith. It's as if GOD tells you, "I'M going to bless you and your family. But, MY ultimate goal is to bless everybody on your block.

- Once I bless everybody on your block, I want to bless everybody in your city.
- Once I bless everyone in your city, I want to bless everyone in your state.
- Once I bless everyone in your state, it's MY goal to bless everyone in your country.
- Once you become blessed as a country, I hope to reach those in other nations.

GOD says, "Now I know there's going to be somebody that's going to reject what I have to offer. But, by the time I bless all those who choose to be blessed, at least the whole world would have at least had a chance to be blessed. And, it all started with the promise I made to you!"

Verse 16, *For if the first fruit is holy, the lump is also holy; and if the root is holy, so are the branches.* Because we are connected to Abraham's faith, we're also connected to Abraham's promises. That's why the first fruits are always considered holy. What's so amazing about verse 16 is that it is a principle. Look at the text again. *For if the first fruit is holy...*

Even in tithing, the moment I receive an increase, when I set aside what belongs to GOD *first*, that is considered the first fruit. The text says *For if the first fruit is holy, the lump is also holy...* My offerings become holy when I offer GOD the first fruits of my increase and not what's left. Because, I am attached to my offering, look at what the text says *and if the root is holy, so are the branches.* Because Abraham represents the first fruits, GOD considers him holy. Because we connect to Abraham's faith, we are also considered holy since we represent the branches.

That's why if I am saved and I know I am saved. I refuse to allow anyone to still call me a sinner. Especially, if I'm not practicing a lifestyle of sin. People are quick to say, "Well, we are all sinners." My testimony is, "I used to be a sinner. Grace has made me into the righteousness of GOD. I'm one of the branches that have connected to the root which GOD considers holy. Which makes me holy by connection."

Verse 17 is going to explain why only the remnant has obtained favor and not the whole circle. *But some of the olive branches have been broken off, and you, a wild olive branch, have been grafted in their place. You get your nourishment from the roots of the olive tree.* Those who should have received the promise didn't. But, because you are connected to the tree by faith, your faith attached you to the tree, and everything the tree has to offer, you benefit from.

To prove that we benefit from the tree by being attached to it through faith, look at verses 18 – 20. *So don't brag about being better than the other branches. If you brag, remember that you don't support the root, the root supports you. "Well," you say, "Branches were cut off so that I could be grafted onto the tree." That's right! They were broken off because they didn't believe, but you remain on the tree because you do believe. Don't feel arrogant, but be afraid.*

In other words, don't become like the Jews just because you inherited the promise through faith. The Jews' problem was that they looked down on everyone else, because they thought they inherited the promise through their race and not through their faith. Since they didn't have Abraham's faith, Paul said, *They were broken off;* cut off. The fear of being cut off helps me to continue in well-doing and not continue in sins that satisfy my flesh.

The next part of the text is very controversial. Especially, to those that believe "once saved always saved." Look at verses 21 – 22, *If GOD didn't spare the natural branches, HE won't spare you, either. Look at how kind and how severe GOD can be. HE is severe to those who fell, but kind to you if you continue to hold on to HIS kindness. Otherwise, you, too, will be cut off from the tree.*

According to verse 21 and verse 22, let's not focus on our opinion, but solely on what the text says. The text says it is very possible to be cut off. If you continue in HIS goodness and in the faith, you will stay attached to the tree. If you choose not to continue in the faith, otherwise you also will be cut off.

Question. As a Believer that has been saved by grace, why do you think when we fall short it's easy for us to *continue in well-doing*? The HOLY SPIRIT is in us and HE convicts us when we fall short. Because we don't want to disappoint GOD, we beg for forgiveness and repent and strive to live right. Even though grace has freed us from the bondage of sin, the moment we were set free, Paul told us GOD gave us dominion over sin.

Even though we have dominion and authority over sin, it's still our option to exercise that authority. That's why it grieves the HOLY SPIRIT when we give in to the flesh. When we don't exercise that authority, by GOD being in us, not only do we give sin control over our flesh, we give sin authority over us, me and GOD.

This is where the term backslidden comes into play. Remember when Paul talked about us having a spiritual nature and a corrupt nature? As we have learned, our spiritual nature has dominion over our corrupt nature. Even though we have control over our corrupt nature, this does not stop our corrupt nature from wanting to participate in sin.

It's our choice to decide to follow our spirit nature or our corrupt nature. A backslider is someone who has decided to leave the fold and live in the world in a lifestyle of sin. A backslider is not someone who frequently comes to church and chooses to live in sin. When you have backslidden, you have left the fold to go live in sin. Someone who lives in sin, but continues to come to church is someone who was never saved. A backslider is someone who has run away from home. If you are a runaway, you don't come home to eat dinner every night.

A backslider needs to come back home. Someone that comes to church, but still chooses to live in sin needs to get saved. If either were to die in their disorder, they both wouldn't make it into the Kingdom.

Verses 23-24: (NKJV) *And they also, if they do not continue in unbelief, will be grafted in, for GOD is able to graft them in again. For if you were cut out of the olive tree which is wild by nature, and were grafted contrary to nature into a cultivated olive tree, how much more will these, who are natural branches, be grafted into their own olive tree?*

You have two types of reprobates. The backslider who chooses not to return and the one that has a zeal for GOD, but refuses to live for GOD. The latter is the one that comes to church, but still chooses to live in sin.

Let's look at the two according to Scripture. The first one is the backslider. Remember what Romans 1:28 told us, *And even as they did not like to retain GOD in their knowledge, GOD gave them over to a reprobate mind, to do those things which are not convenient.*

The fake believer that attends church, but continues to live in sin was never saved. Titus 1:16, *They profess that they know GOD; but in works they deny HIM, being abominable, and disobedient, and unto every good work reprobate.* These are in church. They are doing the work of the Believer and claim to know GOD. You can tell they don't belong to GOD because of how they live; they deny GOD. Their lifestyle is sinful and disobedient.

That's why Paul said in verse 20, instead of being arrogant because we are now saved, we need to be afraid. Our sinful nature will always try to separate us from GOD. If we backslide and our sin disconnects us from GOD, verse 22 says, *otherwise, you also will be cut off.* GOD only disconnects us when we become reprobate.

I'm almost sure that's a scary feeling when you know you have left the fold and allowed your sins, that you were delivered from, to disconnect you from GOD. I can't imagine being covered by GOD, but feel like I have gone too far away from GOD. I'm sure there has to be something in the back of a

Believer's mind that constantly reminds them they have gone too far. That's why we have a rededication. It's for those that have left the fold and gone back into the world. That's why verse 23 said *if they do not continue in unbelief, will be grafted in, for GOD is able to graft them in again.* What's the keyword in verse 23? Again.

Remember, Paul told us GOD's initial plan was to save mankind through the promise HE made to Abraham and his seeds. A lot of Jews *were cut off the tree because they didn't believe, but you remain on the tree because you do believe.*

Verse 25, *For I do not desire, brethren, that you should be ignorant of this mystery, lest you should be wise in your own opinion, that blindness in part has happened to Israel until the fullness of the Gentiles has come in. And so all Israel will be saved, as it is written: "The Deliverer will come out of Zion, and He will turn away ungodliness from Jacob; For this is My covenant with them, When I take away their sins."*

Paul is telling the new converts, that just because GOD cut the Jews off, those who chose not to believe, don't start looking down on them because they were cut off. Remember the initial plan; to save the world. Hopefully, by saving the world, those who thought they were entitled to GOD by race will now become saved by faith. Hopefully, those who received the promise will now embrace the promise. Once they see that it's all about faith and not about race, hopefully, they will embrace the faith. GOD says, "When I make a promise, I keep MY promises." Look at what Paul says in verse 29. *For the gifts and the calling of GOD are irrevocable.* The promise still stands. You have to have faith to get them.

Verses 30 – 32, *For as you were once disobedient to GOD, yet have now obtained mercy through their disobedience, even so these also have now been disobedient, that through the mercy shown you they also may obtain mercy. For GOD has committed them all to disobedience, that HE might have mercy on all.* Once again, HIS initial plan is to save all through the promise HE made to Abraham.

Paul says, "So, now the roles have been reversed." GOD says, "At first, you all rejected ME, because of the promise I made to Abraham and his seeds. It has now caused you who had rejected ME to now want to accept ME. So, by taking the promise away from those to who I made the promise and now have given the promise, hopefully, they'll want to be saved also."

It's something about seeing GOD's favor and blessings on someone else. It makes you want to operate in that same favor. The question is, what are you willing to sacrifice to receive this type of favor? A lot of people want it, but a lot of people are not willing to pay the sacrifice to get it. Also, a lot of people want to go to heaven, but a lot of people are not willing to live right to get there.

When I want the promise, but am not willing to do what it takes to get the promise, then I have to establish my own set of rules to make me feel as if I'm still entitled to the promise. That's why some people live by their righteousness. It still gives them a sense of entitlement to GOD's promises. That's what a lot of the Jews did. Once again, they made the promises of GOD about race instead of faith. They didn't want to live by faith. They felt entitled to GOD's promises because of their race.

Verse 29 told us GOD doesn't change HIS mind regarding HIS promises. If GOD's gifts are irreversible, so is HIS covenant. HE is not going to change HIS covenant because we choose not to follow it. What a lot of people don't realize is that GOD doesn't get in line with our plan. We have to get in line with HIS! Like I said before, some want HIS promises, but under their conditions. Paul says, "That is not going to happen." GOD will give HIS promises to someone else who is willing to follow HIS plan before HE rewrites HIS covenant. GOD will adopt someone who does. No sin is worth losing HIS promises.

Verses 33 – 36, *GOD's riches, wisdom, and knowledge are so deep that it is impossible to explain HIS decisions or to understand HIS ways.* "Who knows how the LORD thinks? Who can become HIS adviser?" Who gave the LORD something which the LORD must payback? Everything is from HIM and by HIM and for HIM. Glory belongs to HIM forever! Amen!

GOD's promises are never about us. They are all about HIM! GOD blesses us so HE can get the glory! If GOD promises are never about us, but always about HIM, then why would HE change HIS covenant just because of us? The worst thing a person can do is think that GOD owes them something. Verse 35 asked the question *Who gave the LORD something which the LORD must payback?*

RECAP

We have gone from Romans 1 to Romans 11. Before we enter into chapter 12, let's recap. Romans 1 – 8 taught us about GOD's righteousness being revealed and how to identify a true Believer based on GOD's righteousness. Romans 9 – 11 talked about how Israel rejected GOD's righteousness. They rejected GOD's righteousness and HIS promises. We have been discussing how GOD wants to restore Israel by giving the promise to anyone who chooses to believe by faith.

After chapter 11, Romans takes another shift in chapter 12 through chapter 16 which will give us practical applications. Chapters 12 through 16 talk about examples of how to apply GOD's righteousness and the benefits of walking in HIS righteousness. They are going to teach us the most reasonable, thoughtful and spiritual thing we can do as Believers; to give ourselves to GOD and to live for HIM.

When we follow these principles, we will start finding our lives changing in our relationships. In other words, you will understand why you should love your enemies and do good to those who have done you wrong. These principles will not only bless your enemies, but they will also become more of a blessing to you. Not only will it bring peace to you, but it will bring glory to GOD. Even in your inner self, your attitude will become different.

These principles will cause your attitude to change towards those who disagree with you and hold different values than you whereby it will no longer frustrate or bother you. The principles in chapters 12 through 16 should give you a passion for them.

If you don't want to be a better Believer, then chapters 12 through 16 are not going to be for you. If you want to have inner peace and understanding in all the craziness that surrounds you, then chapters 12 through 16 are going to bless you if you apply the principles. These chapters are going to show us why we should apply everything we learned in chapters 1 through 11 in our lives.

Chapter 12
A Life Dedicated

Dedicate Your Lives to GOD
Verses 1-29

The next few chapters are going to be applications. When you follow these principles, you will find your life starting to change. Especially, with the people around you. Let's venture into chapter 12. The first thing chapter 12 verse 1 instructs us to do is, *I beseech you therefore, brethren, by the mercies of GOD, that you present your bodies a living sacrifice, holy, acceptable to GOD, which is your reasonable service.*

Paul says, "In light of everything we have been talking about, here's what is required of you; *...present your bodies* as *a living sacrifice, holy* so it can be *acceptable to GOD*.

For me to present my body to GOD, there has to be a sacrifice. If my body is going to be GOD's dwelling place, there are some things I have to get rid of for HIM to dwell in my temple. If there is a lot of sin in my temple, I can't present my temple to GOD. Our temples do not have to be perfect. However, they do have to be holy and acceptable.

For GOD to dwell in my temple, Paul said it has to be *holy*. Watch what Paul says. This is not a suggestion. This is a requirement. The only way for GOD to dwell in our temples is, we have to present our temples to HIM as holy. If there are a lot of things going on in our temple, the only way to make our temple holy is by getting rid of stuff that's not holy. Getting rid of it is going to be a sacrifice, but it will be worth the sacrifice.

I will give up lying or a bad attitude for GOD's favor any day! I will give up any sin for GOD's presence any day! If there is a whole lot of stuff taking place in my temple that's not holy, then GOD can't dwell in it.

Question. What are some things that could make our body/our temple not acceptable to GOD? Remember what Paul said in chapter 11:36, *Everything is from GOD and by GOD and for GOD. Why? Glory belongs to GOD.* Anything that will hinder GOD from receiving the glory, such as sin, being unhealthy and certain things we put in our body, can and will make our temple unacceptable.

How can GOD dwell in our temple if we are constantly allowing sin to live in it? HE can't! Paul said the only way for GOD to accept our body, is that it has to be holy. Once again, we have to be willing to live right. We have to live according to HIS righteousness and not our own. We can't try to justify any lifestyle. If our lifestyle is not holy, then GOD is not going to dwell in a corrupted temple.

Do you think that's a lot for GOD to ask of us? Paul did say it will be a sacrifice. If you want GOD to reside in your Temple, you have to be willing to sacrifice and let HIM inside. I don't think it's too much for us to sacrifice our bodies when GOD sacrificed HIS SON. HIS sacrifice cost a lot more than me just saying no to sin. His sacrifice cost Him His life. Our sacrifice only costs us to give up sin.

Let's understand this. The moment we become saved, our body/our temples then become GOD's Temple, right? How we take care of HIS Temple depends on us. HE's only going to dwell in a clean Temple. Look at the wording that Paul uses. Paul said to present our bodies to GOD as a living sacrifice. If you own a piece of property, you are supposed to make sure that property is presentable if you want somebody to move into it. The moment we become saved, our body/our temples become property where GOD's SPIRIT can now dwell. When GOD decides to come to look at our property to see if HE wants to reside in it, how are you presenting your property? When we allow certain things to come in, it can make GOD leave the premises.

I remember when I was in college. There was this thing we used to do whenever we didn't want our roommate to come into the room. We would tie something on the doorknob. When our roommates came to the room and saw something tied to the doorknob, they knew not to come in. The question is, what sin have you tied on the doorknob so GOD can't come in? GOD is not going to come in until you remove the sin.

Verse 2, *And do not be conformed to this world, but be transformed by the renewing of your mind, that you may prove what is that good and acceptable and perfect will of GOD. Paul says do not be conformed to this world. How are you decorating GOD's Temple? Don't decorate GOD's Temple to resemble the world.* When you decorate your temple with worldly things, it is no longer holy. GOD can't dwell in a worldly decorated temple. HE can only dwell in a Holy Temple. When the world can see more of them in you than they can see the GOD in you, then your temple resembles the world. To make our temples holy for GOD to reside in it, we have to be willing to sacrifice our bodies so they can become holy and acceptable to GOD.

After Paul says, *do not be conformed to this world*, watch what he goes on to say in verse 2, *but be transformed by the renewing of your mind*. The only way to know how to decorate our bodies as GOD's Temple is by being *transformed by the renewing of your mind*. This is why we should not judge people that do not look like us when they come to church.

Paul says in verse 2, that as Believers, we're not supposed to resemble the world. If we renew our minds, it will transform our resemblance. Once you renew your mind, it will transform your appearance. Once you renew your mind, it will change what you allow in your temple. It begins with your mind.

How can we demand anyone change their appearance if their mind hasn't been renewed? When you change your mind, it will change your appearance. Paul says, "You are transformed by the renewing of your mind." Here's the benefit of renewing your mind. Verse 2 he is telling us that after our minds are renewed we will then be able to determine what GOD really wants—what is good, pleasing, and perfect.

When we look worldly, it's because our mind is worldly. You only resemble what's in your mind. When you resemble the world, the world will identify you with them and not with GOD. Understand the flow of the text. The only way I can determine what GOD wants, what's pleasing and acceptable to GOD is by the *renewing* of my mind. Once my mind is renewed, it will transform what I decide to present before GOD. Once my mind is renewed, it will transform the way I present myself to the world. Once my mind is renewed, my actions are no longer worldly, but they become holy. My lifestyle is no longer worldly, it is holy.

Once you are *transformed by the renewing of your mind*, when the world sees you, they should be able to see GOD and not a resemblance of themselves. Why? You're not cussing like the world, sinning like the world, nor behaving like the world. Why? Because, *greater is HE that is in you, than he that is in the world.* (1st John 4:4) If HE is in me, then I should resemble HIM and not have worldly behavior. GOD is only going to dwell in temples that resemble HIM and not worldly behaviors. That's why Paul says it's required that every Believer present their temple as a living sacrifice, holy and acceptable to GOD.

That's why I don't have time to focus on what you need to clean in your temple. It's enough work just trying to keep my temple clean and presentable. A lot of people like to focus on what needs to be cleaned in other people's temples so they don't have to deal with what they need to clean in their own temple.

Why is it going to be such a sacrifice, even as a Believer that's been saved by grace? Yes, as a Believer, I have authority over my flesh, but our bodies are used to doing worldly things than spiritual things. That is why Paul says in 1st Corinthians 9:27 *But I discipline my body and bring it into subjection.* The good news is, that Romans 8:26 told us that the HOLY SPIRIT will help us in our time of weakness.

Now, remember we said chapters 12 through 16 are mostly about application, meaning applying. Here's the problem with most of the people in the Church. After they become saved and start cleaning their temples, they start looking at the dirt in everybody else's temple. Verse 3, *Because of the kindness that GOD has shown me, I ask you not to think of yourselves more highly than you should. Instead, your thoughts should lead you to use good judgment based on what GOD has given each of you as believers.*

I sacrifice and clean my house so GOD can dwell in my house. Not clean my house to start judging what's in other people's houses. That's why 2nd Corinthians 13:5 says *Examine yourselves as to whether you are in the faith. Test yourselves. Do you not know yourselves, that JESUS CHRIST is in you?—unless indeed you are disqualified.* Before I go judging what's in your house, I need to make sure my house is presentable to GOD.

Verses 4 and 5 is Paul's way of validating why we shouldn't judge others unrighteous. If there is a need to, it should always be according to GOD's righteousness and not our own righteousness or opinions. Look at what he says. *Our bodies have many parts, but these parts don't all do the same thing. In the same way, even though we are many individuals, CHRIST makes us one body and individuals who are connected to each other.* Even though we are all part of the same body, we all serve different purposes.

If you are the hand and someone else is the feet, how can the hand tell the feet what it is supposed to be doing? The last person to tell the feet what they should be doing is the hand. The last person that can tell the hand what it's supposed to be doing is the elbow. If someone's purpose is to be the elbow, then guess what they're good at? Elbowing.

If someone is the foot, guess what they have been designed to do? Walk, stand, run and jump. How is the elbow going to tell the foot how to walk, stand, run or jump? It can't. The elbow wasn't made for either. The only thing the elbow knows about is bending and rotating. Even if the elbow told the feet how they should walk, it would be giving the feet the wrong information, because the reason the elbow was designed was to bend and rotate and not to walk. The worst thing the foot could do is to take advice from the elbow.

Paul says in other words, "Worry about yourself." If we see a Believer falling short, it's our job to restore that Believer by judging them righteously. Meaning, judge them according to the Scriptures and not our personal opinions. Notice how Paul chooses to use his words. He says, *Our bodies have many parts, but these parts don't all do the same thing. And, CHRIST makes us one body...* Basically, the Body of CHRIST is not made up of a whole bunch of feet, elbows or heads. Each part of the body has its purpose. One part of the body cannot tell the other part of the body what it should be doing because each part has its purpose in the body.

Verses 6-8, *GOD in HIS kindness gave each of us different gifts. If your gift is speaking GOD's Word, make sure what you say agrees with the Christian faith. If your gift is serving, then devote yourself to serving. If it is teaching, devote yourself to teaching. If it is encouraging others, devote yourself to giving encouragement. If it is sharing, be generous. If it is leadership, lead enthusiastically. If it is helping people in need, help them cheerfully.*

Not only are we supposed to worry about our assignment, but it is equally important to be doing our assignment. If you are the only one equipped, designed, and intended to operate that particular body part, then that means no one else can do your part but you. If the hand is not doing its part, because the hand thinks there are other hands, then the elbow has to try to do the hand's job when the elbow was not equipped nor designed to do that part. Stepping back or choosing not to do anything makes CHRIST's Body dysfunctional. That's why Paul says if your gift is to do a certain part, then do your part. No one else can do your part but you.

How can I be a part of CHRIST's Body and not be concerned about me doing my part which makes His Body look dysfunctional? If I am a part of The Body, how can I not be concerned that my not doing my part makes

CHRIST's Body looks dysfunctional? Paul said every Believer has a special place in CHRIST's Body. The last thing I would want to do is to be the cause of making CHRIST's Body look dysfunctional. Which we already discussed in *Let's Talk about The Book of Ephesians.*

Look at what Paul instructs us to do in verses 9-11. *Love sincerely. Hate evil. Hold on to what is good. Be devoted to each other like a loving family. Excel in showing respect for each other. Don't be lazy in showing your devotion. Use your energy to serve the Lord.* Instead of fighting each other in the Body of CHRIST, Paul said we should *devote* yourselves *to each other* like *family* by *showing respect for each other*. How do the hands show *respect* to the feet? By allowing the feet to do what it was designed to do. We show *respect* to each other by allowing each other to do what GOD designed each other to do.

After Paul tells us to respect each other gifts, look at what he says in verse 11. *Don't be lazy in showing your devotion. Use your energy to serve the Lord.* If you are designed to be the feet, use all your energy walking, jumping and skipping. Whatever the feet were designed to do, use all your energy doing that. When you do what you were designed to do, it makes the Body of CHRIST effective, productive and useful. It causes you *to serve the LORD*. Paul says *Use your energy to serve the LORD*. When you are doing your part in The Body, you are serving the LORD. If I just focus on my temple, making sure it's presentable for GOD to dwell in, and focus on what my job is in the Body of CHRIST, I don't have time to focus on no one else.

Verses 12 and 13, *Be happy in your confidence, be patient in trouble, and pray continually. Share what you have with GOD's people who are in need.* Be hospitable. Watch how Paul put all this together. He says, "When the Body of CHRIST is functional, functioning properly, CHRIST's Body is then able to serve those who stand in need." The flip side is, that when The Body is dysfunctional, it is not meeting the needs of those who are in need. I don't want to be the one responsible for CHRIST's Body not meeting the needs of those who are in need. The one causing The Body to be dysfunctional by being *lazy*.

These principles in the last verses will not only bless those around us, but they will also bless us as well. Look at verses 14 through 21, *Bless those who persecute you. Bless them, and don't curse them. Be happy with those who are happy. Be sad with those who are sad. Live in harmony with each other. Don't be arrogant, but be friendly to humble people. Don't think that you are smarter than you really are. Don't pay people back with evil for the evil they do to you. Focus your thoughts on those things that are considered noble. As much as it is possible, live in peace with everyone. Don't take revenge, dear friends. Instead, let GOD's anger take care of it. After all, Scripture says, "I alone have the right to take revenge. I will pay back, says the Lord." But, "If your enemy is hungry, feed him. If he is thirsty, give him a drink. If you do this, you will make him feel guilty and ashamed." Don't let evil conquer you, but conquer evil with good.*

How does doing all of this bless us? I'm glad you asked. Evil begets and causes evil. When someone persecutes me, I don't help the situation by persecuting them. Evil plus evil equals more evil; (1+1=2). Evil minus evil cancels out; (1-1=0). It's basic arithmetic.

Look at what Paul says in verse 14. *Bless those*, positive (+) *who persecute you*, negative (-). Then look at what he says in verse 15. *Be happy*, positive (+) *with those who are happy*, positive (+). When you get a negative, add a positive so the negative can cancel out. When you get a positive, add a positive so you can increase the positive. But never add a negative to a negative because you will increase the negative. Why escalate a situation when verse 19 GOD says HE *alone have the right to take revenge*. Our job, as Believers, is to always add a positive. That way we will cancel out the negative or we will add to the positive.

Chapter 13

The Government & Love One Another

Obey the Government
Verses 1-6

As we enter chapter 13, we see a shift in the application. Let's see what this shift is for us, as Believers, to apply. Verses 1 and 2, *Every person should obey the government in power. No government would exist if it hadn't been established by GOD. The governments which exist have been put in place by GOD. Therefore, whoever resists the government opposes what GOD has established. Those who resist will bring punishment on themselves.*

The shift goes from dedicating our lives to GOD to obeying the government. I hope you don't think this is about the government. It's about respecting GOD's establishment. Whatever GOD has established, should always be respected. Remember in chapter 12, Paul talked about us respecting each other. How do we respect each other? By allowing each person to do their part. I'm not trying to tell you how to do your part. I'm too busy focusing on doing my part.

GOD has a real big issue about staying in your lane. It's when we get out of our lane and into someone else's lane that causes confusion. And according to the text, sometimes destruction. Even with the government, Paul says, "GOD has established government. Just because we have dedicated ourselves to GOD and are now servants of GOD doesn't permit us to disobey the establishment of government."

The reason Paul had to bring this to our attention is that GOD knew the moment we established ourselves under HIS law, we, as Believers, were going to ignore any other laws. Which could be dangerous. For example, since I am a Believer under GOD's Law, if I feel I don't have to obey the speed limit law and can drive as fast as I want, not only will I put my life in jeopardy, I put other people's lives in jeopardy as well. Even with me being a child of the Most High GOD, I still have to obey the speed limit. Just because I'm a child of GOD doesn't exempt me from obeying the speed limit.

Verse 1 says, GOD has established government. When we don't seek GOD regarding government, we allow corrupt people into the government. Even though evil and corrupt people are involved in the government, Paul says GOD only established the system; no matter what corrupt people enter the government. Since GOD established it, GOD is still involved in HIS establishment. HE may not control the government, but HE is always involved in it.

That's why the book of Acts 5:29 tells us when the government tries to make us go against GOD, then as Believers, we have the right to say we will obey GOD. *Peter and the other apostles answered, "We must obey GOD rather than people.* When the government is right, we obey that which is right. When the government is wrong, we obey GOD. Simple!

Same way with marriage. GOD established the institution of marriage. As always, man will try to change what GOD has established. When man tries to add sin to what GOD has established, then we have the right to obey GOD. The only law Believers don't have to tolerate is the law of sin. When sin enters into GOD's establishment, we don't have to follow sin just because someone put it in the law.

Here's how a corrupted government tries to get Believers to follow the law of sin; by referring to that sin as a law and not a sin. As if the moment it becomes a law, it is no longer a sin. Sin is sin. Even if it has been made into a law. Any law that hasn't been tainted by sin, as Believers, we have to respect it.

Here's the danger for those who get into government and then allow sin to enter into GOD's establishment. They are going to be in big trouble! Watch this, even if they are not a Believer. GOD says, "I created the establishment." Same way as marriage. GOD established the institution of marriage. You don't have to be a Believer to get married. The minute you corrupt HIS institution with sin, you have just brought punishment upon yourself. Proverbs 16:22 *It is an abomination for kings to commit wickedness. For a throne is established by righteousness.*

Anyone who holds a position of authority in GOD's establishment, GOD holds them to some level of accountability. Whether they believe in GOD or not. Why? It's HIS establishment. As Believers, we respect the government, not because of who holds a position in government. We respect it, since it is GOD's establishment.

Verses 3-5, *People who do what is right don't have to be afraid of the government. But people who do what is wrong should be afraid of it. Would you like to live without being afraid of the government? Do what is right, and it will praise you. The government is GOD's servant working for your good. But if you do what is wrong, you should be afraid. The government has the right to carry out the death sentence. It is GOD's servant, an avenger to execute GOD's anger on anyone who does what is wrong. Therefore, it is necessary for you to obey, not only because you're afraid of GOD's anger but also because of your own conscience.*

You can become so religious and feel as if the government does not apply to you. If you break its law, it has the authority to give you consequences. If you run the red light and get caught, you get a ticket. If you rob a bank, you go to jail. Don't get mad at GOD because you have to deal with the consequences of disobeying the law. To go against the government is also going against GOD's establishment. Not only will you be sinning, but you have to deal with the consequence of breaking the law.

Now, I hate to do this to you, but since it's in the text, I'm obligated to give it to you. Look at verse 6. *That is also why you pay your taxes. People in the government are GOD's servants while they do the work HE has given them.* The moment you become a part of GOD's institution, whether you are a Believer or not, you are now considered a servant of GOD. Here's what GOD established. When you are involved in the government, you are employed by GOD to serve HIS people. Same way in the Kingdom of GOD. Any position held in the Kingdom is employed by GOD to serve HIS people.

The government is GOD's physical establishment. While the Kingdom is GOD's spiritual establishment. Since they are both GOD's establishments, they are both supposed to operate in the same manner by serving HIS people. The moment you bring sin and corruption into either of HIS establishments, you have just brought abomination upon yourself.

That's why those who are corrupt tried to separate church and state. They didn't want to be held to GOD's standards. Even if you separate them, guess what? They still belong to GOD, since HE established them.

Love One Another
Verses 7-14

Verses 7 and 8, *Pay everyone whatever you owe them. If you owe taxes, pay them. If you owe tolls, pay them. If you owe someone respect, respect that person. If you owe someone honor, honor that person. Pay your debts as they come due. However, one debt you can never finish paying is the debt of love that you owe each other. The one who loves another person has fulfilled Moses' Teachings.*

It is wrong to accumulate debt and not pay it back. Especially, if you are a child of GOD. That's why verse 8 tells us to owe no man anything. When we belong to GOD, and we have debt we can't pay back that makes our DADDY looks bad. Could you imagine me being a billionaire and my son has all these little bitty debts he owes other people? That makes me look bad as his father. It appears as if I'm stingy. Especially, if I have established him away to be debt-free. To owe no one anything.

GOD says, "How are you going to be in debt when your FATHER owns the heavens and the universe?" Here you are with a rich DADDY, in $200 worth of debt. Where do they do that at? How are you going to be bragging about your DADDY being rich in houses and land, but you're in debt and always borrowing?

Don't get me wrong. And, don't misinterpret the text. The text is not saying you have to have a lot of stuff to prove who GOD is. The text is saying owe no man. Meaning, that you don't have to keep borrowing, because you're always struggling. The moment you borrow, you are now in debt. Why do I have to keep borrowing, when all I have to do is trust my

DADDY?

Paul says, "The only debt you should never be able to pay off is love." Most people feel that just because they have shown love to one person, then their account is clear. "I have shown love to this person. So, I'm free to cuss another person out!" Paul says we are forever indebted to showing love. Meaning, that it's our responsibility to show love at all times and to everybody. Even those that hate you and have done you wrong.

Watch how Paul so eloquently put all this together to make sense. Paul says in verse 8 that when you love one another you have fulfilled the law, right? Now, look at what Paul says in verse 9. *The commandments, "Never commit adultery; never murder; never steal; never have wrong desires," and every other commandment are summed up in this statement: "Love your neighbor as you love yourself."*

- Do you want to know why someone would commit adultery? It's because they didn't love their spouse.

- You want to know why someone would commit murder? It's because they didn't love the person they murdered.

- You want to know why someone would steal? It's because they didn't love the person they stole from. Surely you wouldn't steal from somebody you loved.

- You want to know why it's easy for some people to lie on someone else? They don't love that person. Surely, you wouldn't bear false witness on someone you love.

- You want to know why it's easy to want something that belongs to someone else? They don't love that person. If I love you, why would

I want to take something that belongs to you?

Verse 10, *Love never does anything that is harmful to a neighbor. Therefore, love fulfills Moses' Teachings.* You can come up with your own interpretation of love to justify you doing these things to other people. However, according to the Bible, this type of love never does these types of things to anyone or anything they love. The only way these things can be done is because there is no love. A lot of people have confused a strong like to love.

When you examine like and love, there is a major difference. Let's understand the difference. When somebody likes you. Know this to be true, for them to like you, they like you 'because of.' They like you for a reason. When people fall in love with liking you, what happens is, that you have to continue to do whatever you did for them to like you. When whatever you were doing runs out, their liking runs out also. Everybody has a reason for liking you. If you want them to continue to like you, you must continue doing what you did for them to like you.

Love is a lot different than like. When you take love and put it under the microscope, the difference between love and like is, like stands up and says, "I like you 'because of'." Love stands up and says, "I love you 'in spite of'." Love is an action word. Love is what you do, not something you say. When JESUS asked Peter three times in John 21, *Simon, son of Jonah, do you love Me?* What JESUS was saying to Peter was, "Don't just tell Me you love ME. Show ME you love ME by your actions. Don't talk like you love ME. Walk as you love ME. If your talking doesn't match your walking, you don't love ME like you say you love ME."

People are more comfortable saying "love" than doing it. If you're not willing to do love, you shouldn't say it. That is why Paul tells us in verse 8, "The debt of love that we owe each other, we can never finish paying. When we show love to each other, we have *fulfilled Moses' Teachings.*

It seems like when Paul wrote these last verses in chapter 13, it was meant for us today. The application part is in verses 13 – 14. But, the reason why we should apply it is in verses 11 – 12. After Paul tells us in verse 10, *Love never does anything that is harmful to a neighbor*, in verses 11 and 12 he says *You know the times in which we are living. It's time for you to wake up. Our salvation is nearer now than when we first became Believers. The night is almost over, and the day is near. So we should get rid of the things that belong to the dark and take up the weapons that belong to the light.*

For some reason, a lot of sin happens at night. Night has gotten a bad rap; a lot of things go on at night or in the darkness. Whenever someone participates in sin, Paul considers it darkness. Not only does sin represents darkness, but a lot of people like to sleep in the dark.

When you take sleep in verse 11 and sin in verse 12 and put them together, they equal darkness. Paul says, "Because a lot of people are participating in sin, they are sleeping. Not realizing that it's about to be day." The problem is, they're living their life as if they are still in the dark and it's light outside.

As Believers, what we don't want to get caught doing is living in the dark, during the day. A lot of people are living in the dark during the day and they care less who sees them sleeping, during the day!

Since no one knows *that day and hour, not even the angels of heaven, but the FATHER only*, Paul was reminding the Romans how serious it was to present their bodies as living sacrifices so they would be holy and acceptable to GOD. (Matthew 24:36, Romans 12:1) Even if the Day of Judgement is 3,000 years from now, I don't have 3,000 years to present my body holy and acceptable. Whatever my death date is, that is how long I have. Since, none of us knows that date, *Behold, now is the accepted time; behold, now is the day of salvation.* (2nd Corinthians 6:2)

If today is the day of salvation, in verse 13, Paul tells us what we should and what we shouldn't be doing as Believers right now! Not tomorrow. Not next week. Not when we feel it's the right time, but right now! *We should live decently, as people who live in the light of day. Wild parties, drunkenness, sexual immorality, promiscuity, rivalry, and jealousy cannot be part of our lives.*

Paul says it's time for the Believers to wake up and stop sleeping during the day and participating in sin like it was night. If these sins (*Wild parties, drunkenness, sexual immorality, promiscuity, rivalry, and jealousy...*) represent darkness, there are a whole lot of people walking in the dark, during the day.

Instead of the Believers walking around like sinning zombies, during the day, in verse 14 Paul says *Instead*, we should *live like the Lord JESUS CHRIST did, and forget about satisfying the desires of your sinful nature.* As a Believer, the same way we walk during the day should be the same way we're supposed to walk during the night. We're not supposed to bring darkness into the day. We are supposed to bring the light into the night by living right. By not satisfying the desires of our sinful nature. If we continue to *live like the Lord JESUS CHRIST did,* not only will it be helpful, but it will also be rewarding.

Like the writer told the Hebrews Believers in Hebrews 10:23. I, Melvin King, also say to you, *Let us hold fast the confession of our hope without wavering, for HE who promised is faithful.* If you know GOD is faithful, you can shout right now!

Chapter 14
Strengthen the Weak

How to Treat Christians Who Are Weak in Faith
Verses 1-23

In chapter 14, Paul does something very strategic. He talks about, 'how to treat Christians who are weak in the faith'. Did you notice how strategically Paul attached chapter 14 to chapter 13? He opens up chapter 14, talking about 'helping those who are weak in the faith', right after he just talked about the flesh having a problem with lust. Paul knew there were going to be Believers that were going to have issues with their flesh.

Remember what Paul told us in chapter 13 verse 14. *The night is almost over, and the day is near. So we should get rid of the things that belong to the dark and take up the weapons that belong to the light.* If we get comfortable satisfying our flesh at night, we won't care about what our flesh is doing during the day. Paul wanted to wake their flesh up before it becomes day. Those who are weak in their faith. Those who were struggling in the faith found it hard to *get rid of the things that belong to the dark.*

When we enter verse 1, he tells us to *Welcome people who are weak in faith, but don't get into an argument over differences of opinion.* The first thing we must do as Believers is welcome those who are weak in the faith. Those who have a struggle. We are supposed to welcome them and not reject them. Welcome them and not criticize them.

Look at who Paul is talking about. He's talking about those who are weak in the faith and not unbelievers. He's talking about the Believers who are sleeping in their darkness. It's our job to try to wake them before the day. The only way to awaken them is, we have to be willing to welcome them. Do you know how many people remain in their sinful behavior because we as Believers refuse to welcome them? For some reason, we think by welcoming those means accepting their lifestyle and behavior.

Paul says after we are supposed to welcome them, he says we're not supposed to get into an argument over differences of opinions. If I'm awake and they are asleep, why would I argue with someone who is sleeping? It's my job as their brother in CHRIST to try to wake them out of their sleep so they can eventually see the light. I can't help wake them up if I am arguing over differences of opinions with them. I can only wake them if I'm willing to welcome them.

Now, don't misinterpret what Paul is saying. When Paul says welcome them who are weak in the faith, he's not saying accept their behavior. What he's saying is, that when we welcome them, it causes us not to criticize them because of our differences. We're supposed to be awake while they are sleeping. The moment we learn how to put our differences aside and welcome the Believer and not their behavior, the Believer can get help from their behavior. The Believer will never get help from their behavior if we keep rejecting the Believer because of their behavior. Reject the behavior, not the Believer. Help and welcome the Believer.

In verses 2 through 4, *Some people believe that they can eat all kinds of food. Other people with weak faith believe that they can eat only vegetables. People who eat all foods should not despise people who eat only vegetables. In the same way, the vegetarians should not criticize people who eat all foods, because GOD has accepted those people. Who are you to criticize someone else's servant? The Lord will determine whether HIS servant has been successful. The servant will be successful because the Lord makes him successful.*

Every Believer belongs to GOD. Whether they are walking in the light or walking in darkness, they are HIS servants. Since they are HIS servants, they belong to HIM. If they belong to HIM, who are we to judge who and what belongs to GOD? Only HE can judge what belongs to HIM. It's our job to help them before it's time for HIM to judge them. Our problem in the Body of CHRIST is, that we can't welcome them, since we are too busy arguing over our differences of opinions in verse 1. We can't get beyond verse 1 *Welcome people who are weak in faith.*

I remember seeing a post that said, "We can't save the world, because we have to keep saving the church." At some point, the church has to wake up. The Believers have to come out of the darkness. This had to be an issue between the Jewish and Gentile Believers in Rome. Verses 5 and 6, *One person decides that one day is holier than another. Another person decides that all days are the same. Every person must make his own decision. When people observe a special day, they observe it to honor the Lord. When people eat all kinds of foods, they honor the Lord as they eat, since they give thanks to GOD. Vegetarians also honor the Lord when they eat, and they, too, give thanks to GOD.*

Paul is not saying that we should ignore or neglect The LORD's Day because it's not important. The LORD's Day is important to GOD. Paul says, "It is the day we honor HIS SON as followers." We shouldn't worship the day. We should honor the ONE who is responsible for all days. Whether you honor GOD on Monday or Tuesday. Whether you thank GOD for your vegetables or meat. We all 'honor the Lord and give thanks to GOD'. Just because someone chooses to honor GOD on a Monday and thank GOD for their vegetables, doesn't make them wrong, because you honor GOD on Tuesday and thank GOD for meat. *Every person must make his own decision.* Based on their decision, *when people observe a special day, they observe it to honor the Lord.*

Paul even simplifies his statement even more in verses 7 through 9. *It's clear that we don't live to honor ourselves, and we don't die to honor ourselves. If we live, we honor the Lord, and if we die, we honor the Lord. So whether we live or die, we belong to the Lord. For this reason, CHRIST died and came back to life so that He would be the Lord of both the living and the dead.* Wow!

When we honor GOD while we are living, we also honor HIM in death. A lot of people think they can only honor GOD while living. Paul says *If we live, we honor the Lord, and if we die, we honor the Lord.*

Someone may be wondering, how can we honor GOD in death? When our faith is in CHRIST, GOD takes our faith and identifies us with the crucifixion and the resurrection of CHRIST. When CHRIST was crucified and resurrected, He became the Lord of the living and the dead. He is the same LORD of both those living here on Earth and those who are absent from the body and is present with GOD. *So, whether we live or die, we belong to the Lord.* That alone is worth rejoicing!

Verse 10 (NKJ) *But why do you judge your brother? Or why do you show contempt for your brother? For we shall all stand before the judgment seat of CHRIST.* The God's Word translation says *Why do you criticize or despise other Christians? Everyone will stand in front of GOD to be judged.* Paul says we spend way too much time judging and criticizing each other instead of helping each other. To be honest, the only time we're supposed to *shake the dust* is when those who are not changing start causing us to participate in their behavior. (Matthew 10:14)

If helping you is starting to hurt me, it's time to shake the dust! If trying to pull you out starts to pull me in, since you have no desire of getting out, then I'm supposed to shake the dust before you pull both of us in. But other than that, as Believers, we're supposed to help and welcome those who are weak in the faith.

I think we need to pause for the cause and discuss this issue. Why do you think it is hard to help those that have fallen short? Mainly because of our differences. I view something one way and because you view it another way, I automatically think you are wrong. Back to verses 5-9.

After Paul tells us in verse 10 that *everyone will stand in front of GOD to be judged,* look at what he says in verses 11-12. *For it is written: "As I live, says the Lord, Every knee shall bow to Me, And every tongue shall confess to GOD."* All of us will have to give an account of ourselves to GOD. Paul says, why are the strong in the faith judging the weak in the faith just because we are strong in the faith? In verse 12 he says, "All of us are going to have to give an account for ourselves to GOD." It's not like we can stand before GOD and tell GOD what somebody else did wrong. You're going to be too busy explaining all the things you did wrong; what you were doing behind closed doors, and what you were doing in the nighttime when no one was looking. No one will have time to give someone else's account.

What's the application? Look at verse 13. *So let's stop criticizing each other. Instead, you should decide never to do anything that would make other Christians have doubts or lose their faith.* Wow! Did y'all catch what Paul said? "Not only are we not supposed to criticize those who are weak in the faith, but criticizing them pushes them further and further away from the faith." Criticizing makes them *lose their faith*.

I don't know about you, but I do not want to be the one responsible for pushing someone out of the faith because I chose not to welcome them back into the faith due to my difference of opinion regarding their behavior. We're supposed to welcome them regardless of our opinion of them. It's our job to try and restore them. I don't want to see a fellow Believer, who was close to the Kingdom, not make it in because of their behavior. Even if someone is an unbeliever and rejects GOD, I still don't want them to go to hell. I hope at some point in their life they will accept GOD and live their life according to HIS Word.

If I don't want to see an unbeliever not make it into the Kingdom, I don't want to see a Believer who's weak in the faith miss heaven because of their behavior. We shouldn't be more concerned about the unbeliever who has flat-out rejected GOD than we are about the Believer who has fallen short. Falling short is possible for every Believer. I don't want anyone to give up on me just because I fell short. Pray for me! Try to strengthen me back into the faith. Remind me of the GOD I serve. Don't neglect me just because you disagree with me.

Verses 14 and 15, *The Lord JESUS has given me the knowledge and conviction that no food is unacceptable in and of itself. But it is unacceptable to a person who thinks it is. So if what you eat hurts another Christian, you are no longer living by love. Don't destroy anyone by what you eat. CHRIST died for that person.* Watch what verse 16 says because it is so important. Don't allow anyone to say that what you consider good is evil.

I know GOD's Word is right. I know HIS Word is life. I know HIS Word is everything I need it to be in my life. Paul says in verse 16, don't be so judgmental, critical, and negative towards someone whereby what you know is good causes someone to consider it evil. That's a lot of damage to that which we know is good. The damage is done when after coming into contact with you, what you know is good, someone else considers evil. For example, if the Word of GOD is going forth in your ministry, and you talk about your ministry to someone else, they should want to come to visit your ministry. If after talking to you their attitude is, "I wouldn't step foot into your ministry." What you know is good, to someone else, you have represented your ministry as evil.

My example was for someone that doesn't go to church. Paul is talking about someone weak in the faith. They should already know what is good. They just need someone to come and remind them of how good it is. If we turn someone from the faith who is weak in the faith and they think the faith is now evil, we have done some major damage to the little faith they were holding on to. We may never get them back into the faith.

That's why Paul starts off chapter 14 in verse 1 by telling us to *Welcome those who are weak in the faith.* For some reason, they are walking on a very thin line. How we as Believers respond to them determines if they come back into the faith and live righteously or if they leave the faith and continue in their sins. I don't want to be the one responsible for kicking someone out of the faith.

Verses 17 and 18 *GOD's Kingdom does not consist of what a person eats or drinks. Rather, GOD's Kingdom consists of GOD's approval and peace, as well as the joy that the HOLY SPIRIT gives. The person who serves CHRIST with this in mind is pleasing to GOD and respected by people.* We don't have time to argue over our minor differences. What's most important is living right and having peace and joy in the HOLY SPIRIT. If I'm living right, which should cause me to have peace and joy in the HOLY SPIRIT, then the HOLY SPIRIT in me is happy. Then HE gives me peace and joy when I come in contact with a Believer who is weak in the faith. How can someone have a conversation with you and leave offended when the HOLY SPIRIT in you is happy with you and give you peace and joy?

We are most offensive when either we are not living right, "So, let me highlight your mess so I can hide my mess." Or we have placed ourselves above them whereby we think we are better than them; our different is different than theirs. Their different is wrong.

In verse 18, Paul says when we don't focus on our differences, *The person who serves CHRIST with this in mind is pleasing to GOD and respected by people.* Here comes the application again in verse 19. *So let's pursue those things which bring peace and which are good for each other.* We are to pursue the things that bring about peace and not confusion. When we pursue peace, not only does it edify and improve them, Paul says it brings *good for each other.*

Verse 20, *Do not destroy the work of GOD for the sake of food. All things indeed are pure, but it is evil for the man who eats with offense.* In other words, don't ruin GOD's work because of our petty differences. When we spend too much time focusing on our differences and petty stuff that causes confusion, it *destroy the work of GOD.* Especially, for the man who eats to be offensive, do things to be offensive, and say things to be offensive. That's what you call being petty. GOD doesn't want us to be petty in our behavior.

Petty behavior will cause someone else to lose their faith.

No matter how wrong they are, no matter how right we may be, never do anything that will cause someone else to stumble in their faith. Especially, someone who is weak in their faith. What can be right for one person may be the downfall for someone else. For example, if I decide to have a glass of wine, I am not sinning. If having a glass of wine is going to turn someone away from the faith, I can have a glass of wine another time.

Question, what are some other examples that could turn someone away from the faith, but maybe totally innocent? Verses 21 and 22, *The right thing to do is to avoid eating meat, drinking wine, or doing anything else that causes another Christian to have doubts. So, whatever you believe about these things, keep it between yourself and GOD. The person who does what he knows is right shouldn't feel guilty. He is blessed.*

If someone considers having a glass of wine a sin, I don't have to feel guilty about having a glass of wine. They may not understand that a glass of wine is not a sin. Because, I don't want to offend them, I'll choose not to have a glass of wine. I don't want to be the man who eats to be offensive. Even if it's not a sin.

The reason Paul teaches us this is that a lot of people lack understanding. If you go into some churches and touched the communion table, they will almost have a heart attack. Because of their lack of understanding, don't offend them by touching the communion table. Even though we know touching the table will not send us to hell. The problem is, that they haven't received the proper teaching.

Verse 23, *But if a person has doubts and still eats, he is condemned because he didn't act in faith. Anything that is not done in faith is sin.* If I know something is not a sin and I know it offends you, Paul says, "You are condemned because you're not acting in faith." In other words, it's our job as Believers to draw into and not drive away. If we intentionally drive someone away, regardless if we are wrong or right, if we know that it will offend someone, we are wrong even though we might be right.

Our right should never come off as offensive. If it offends, our right was not done in faith. If I'm trying to restore you, it should matter to me if I offend you. What did verse 16? Don't let your good be considered evil. I don't want my good to be considered evil. A lot of times when we know that we are right, our attitude is, "We don't care who we offend. I'm right and they are wrong."

Paul says we shouldn't try to offend anyone with the truth. The truth should help and restore. Not offend! Watch this, JESUS never offended anyone HE was trying to help. The only people HE offended were those that didn't want help. Those that didn't want to change, like the Pharisees! He quickly called them hypocrites.

Those HE was trying to help and deliver, like the lady at the well, HE didn't offend her. Even though HE told her about herself, HE restored her. When we take GOD's truth and try to use it to offend people, we take HIS Word and use it as a weapon to hurt and not to help. We use it to destroy and not to build.

GOD says, MY righteousness was never intended to hurt people. It was intended to help and restore people to ME. Some people can be very dangerous when they get a little truth. They try to use GOD's truth to try and prove everybody else wrong. As a Believer, my focus should be on trying to help others live right. Not trying to prove they are wrong.

Once again the application is in verse 19. *So let's pursue those things which bring peace and joy because those are the things that are good for each other.*

Chapter 15
Unity & Paul's Desire

GOD Gives Us Unity
Verses 1-13

After Paul talks to us about helping those who are weak in the faith in chapter 14, he opens up chapter 15 by telling us in verse 1, *So those of us who have a strong faith must be patient with the weaknesses of those whose faith is not so strong. We must not think only of ourselves.* Whenever I come in contact with a Believer, who is weak in the faith, even when I know they are wrong, my attitude should always be about them and not about me. My approach to them should always be to seek a solution that will strengthen them in their faith and not offend them out of the faith.

Verse 2, *We should all be concerned about our neighbor and the good things that will build his faith.* Paul says, "We should be concerned about the things that will build their faith." Not trying to prove them wrong. Verse 3, *CHRIST did not think only of Himself. Rather, as Scripture says, "The insults of those who insult you have fallen on me."* We don't come off offensive so our good won't be looked upon as evil.

When we are trying to restore a fellow Believer, we may have to give up our rights when we know they are wrong. You may have to give up your strength for someone else's weakness. It's our job, as Believers, those who are strong in the faith, to bear the infirmities of those who are weak in the faith. You don't have to prove that you are right and they are wrong. You don't have to prove that they are weak and you are strong. They should see your strength without you trying to prove to them how strong you are.

Paul closes Romans by telling the Believers, "You need to come together. Or should I say, You need to get it together." When the Church comes together, we are more effective. When the devil can get the Believers to fight against each other, then my question is, who is fighting the devil? We know the devil has been defeated. Which means he has no power. As low down and dirty as the devil is, you must admit, he's pretty clever in his ways. If anybody can control you and influence you with power that they don't have, that's pretty clever.

Verse 4 (NKJV), *For whatever things were written before were written for our learning, that we through the patience and comfort of the Scriptures might have hope.* Everything that was written in the Scriptures was written to do what? Verse 4 says it was *written for our learning...through the patience and comfort of the Scriptures*, that's where we'll find our *hope*.

When it comes to trying to restore someone, who may be weak in the faith, they don't need our criticism. Verse 4 tells us their hope is in GOD's Word. Their help and instructions are in GOD's Word. If GOD's Word has patience and comfort until we finally get our stuff together, how are we going to turn around and be impatient and judgmental to someone else?

Verse 5-6, *Now may the GOD of patience and comfort grant you to be like-minded toward one another, according to CHRIST JESUS, that you may with one mind and one mouth glorify the GOD and Father of our Lord JESUS CHRIST.* When Believers come together and get on one accord, GOD can be glorified. A divided church cannot worship GOD. I don't care how much they shout. If there is more confusion going forth than GOD's Word, then GOD is not being glorified. A fighting church is a confused church. GOD is never a part of the confusion. The more we come together, it puts us on one accord. Every time the Believers are on one accord, GOD is always present. Not only is GOD present, but HE is also pleased.

Look at what verses 5 and 6 says when we come together on one accord. Our unity glorifies GOD, because now we resemble HIS SON JESUS. When GOD can see HIS SON in the Believers, HE takes pleasure in the resemblance. The only way we can resemble HIS SON, JESUS, is by being on one accord.

Show me a church that's always fighting. I'll show you a church that not only doesn't resemble CHRIST, but GOD's presence is not present. GOD never visits any place that doesn't resemble HIS SON, JESUS. You don't resemble JESUS by what you say. You resemble HIM by what you do and how you live.

Verse 7, *Therefore receive one another, just as CHRIST also received us, to the glory of GOD.* If CHRIST accepted us, how can we turn around and reject each other? How soon do we forget? Paul is saying, "We should go out of our way to be on one accord." If someone is struggling in the faith, it's the Believers' job not to kick them out of the faith, but try to restore them to the faith. If there is confusion in the faith, we are supposed to *pursue those things which bring peace.* A church united brings glory to GOD. A church divided *destroy the work of GOD.* The Church can accomplish more when we come together on one accord. Every ministry on every corner should be trying to glorify GOD. Not destroying *the work of GOD.*

The more the Church is on one accord, the more it resembles CHRIST. The more the Church resembles CHRIST determines how freely GOD's presence will flow. In verse 8, it shows us a perfect description of the CHRIST we are supposed to resemble. Verse 8, *Now I say that JESUS CHRIST has become a servant to the circumcision for the truth of GOD, to confirm the promises made to the fathers.* Paul says "JESUS became a servant to reveal GOD's truth and to confirm the promises that were made to Abraham, Isaac and Jacob." By Him becoming a servant, not only did it reveal GOD's truth and HIS promises, but look at what verse 9 says. It also *caused others to glorify and trust GOD for HIS promises too.*

Paul is telling us, that there's more that can be done when we come together than it is when the Believers are fighting. The devil, who has no power, has to be pretty brilliant to influence Believers to divide The Church. He knows a church divided will *destroy the work of GOD.*

That's the main reason why I don't allow our ministry to entertain the devil or give him a platform to influence his foolishness. I know a church divided *destroy the work of GOD*. We will not be accused of destroying HIS work. Especially, by someone who has no power. How are you going to give someone a platform to cause division that has no power? Not at Divine Deliverance Ministries! I refuse to allow the devil to use our ministry to *destroy the work of GOD.*

A lot of people like to say, "The devil is busy." Well, guess what? So is GOD! We give the devil too much credit. My attitude is, that the devil can't do anything to me that GOD doesn't allow. If GOD is allowing it, you better believe HE is controlling it.

Verses 10 through 12 talk about what was written in the Old Testament. For it says *"For this reason, I will confess to You among the Gentiles, And sing to Your name." And again he says: "Rejoice, O Gentiles, with His people!" And again: "Praise the Lord, all you Gentiles! Laud Him, all you peoples!" And again, Isaiah says: "There shall be a root of Jesse; And He who shall rise to reign over the Gentiles, In Him, the Gentiles shall hope."*

The next remaining verses are Paul's goodbyes to the Roman Church. The next few verses will show us what made Paul such a great minister of the Gospel.

Paul's Desire to Tell the Good News to the World
Verses 14-33

In verse 13, we see Paul giving his farewell to the Roman Christians in hopes of meeting them one day. For he says, *May GOD, the source of hope, fill you with joy and peace through your faith in HIM. Then you will overflow with hope by the power of the HOLY SPIRIT.*

In verses 14 – 33, Paul talks about his desire to spread the Good News of JESUS CHRIST to the world. Verse 14, *I'm convinced, brothers and sisters, that you, too, are filled with goodness. I'm also convinced that you have all the knowledge you need and that you are able to instruct each other.*

What did you notice about verse 14? Who is this letter written to? The Christians in Rome, right? They weren't Jews. They weren't the Sanhedrin Council. They would be considered Gentiles. Paul refers to them as brothers and sisters. My question is, when did the Body of CHRIST start establishing ranks in the Kingdom? Ranks represent different levels of authority. The different titles in the Bible only distinguished what the Believer did and not who they were in charge of. It established how a Believer would 'serve' in the Kingdom. Not how they should be served.

Verses 15 – 16, *However, I've written you a letter, parts of which are rather bold, as a reminder to you. I'm doing this because GOD gave me the gift to be a servant of CHRIST JESUS to people who are not Jewish. I serve as a priest by spreading the Good News of GOD. I do this in order that I might bring the nations to GOD as an acceptable offering, made holy by the HOLY SPIRIT.*

Those who the Believers attended to were those who labored in the ministry. It wasn't those who held a position. It was the ones that labored and sacrifice for the Kingdom. As a Believer, my position or title should only tell you how I serve in the Kingdom. If your position or title is a prophet, it doesn't place you higher than the pastor. It only says that you are supposed to serve in the Kingdom by delivering a message to the people directly from GOD. If GOD hasn't given you a message to give to HIS people, then sit down and keep your mouth shut until GOD gives you a message; my brother and my sister!

We are so caught up in titles and positions, that we have forgotten our assignments. Every assignment should be used *to equip the saints for the work of ministry. For the building up of the Body of CHRIST until we all attain to the unity of the faith and of the knowledge of the Son of GOD.* (Ephesians 4:12-13) As C.H. Spurgeon says, "If GOD has called you to be HIS servant, don't stoop to be a king." The highest calling on Earth is not being called to be a Bishop, Apostle, Prophet, or Evangelist. The highest calling on Earth is to be a child of the Most High GOD.

Look at what Paul says in verse 16. *I'm here to be a servant of JESUS CHRIST.* Not a commander. Not someone superior, but a servant. Paul says, "My assignment is an Apostle." I am an Apostle servant. Whatever your position is in the Church, put servant behind it. Or maybe, we should put servant in front of our titles to remind us that we are servants first.

In verse 17, Paul says, just in case any of you feel like boasting about your position, he says *So CHRIST JESUS gives me the right to brag about what I'm doing for GOD.* Paul is saying if you want to brag, brag about how many people you brought into the Kingdom. Don't remind us about who you are in the Kingdom. Brag to us about how many people were delivered into the Kingdom. Brag about what you're doing for GOD. GOD calls all of us to serve. If you're not serving, you don't have anything to brag about.

If you are in the choir, don't brag about how good the choir is. Brag once the choir starts bringing people into the Kingdom. That's what you're doing for GOD. Preachers shouldn't brag about how well they can preach. Brag once people are set free from your preaching. If you are impressing them and not impacting them, then you have nothing to brag about. If your position is not bringing anyone into the Kingdom, then you're not doing it for GOD.

Now notice, I didn't say "Bringing people into the church building." I said bringing people into the Kingdom. You can come into the church building one way and leave the same way you came. If you come into the Kingdom, you have to be changed! Anybody can belong to the building, but only those who have been saved and delivered by grace belong to the Kingdom. The church is more concerned about bringing people into the building rather than bringing people into the Kingdom. Why?

We are not concerned about bringing them into the Kingdom. We don't care about them changing their lives in the church. That's why we compete about how many people are in the building; our focus is not on the Kingdom. GOD is trying to build HIS Kingdom, not the neighborhood church. When your focus is on the Kingdom, you are not jealous of how many people are in someone else's building. If people's lives aren't being changed to benefit and increase the Kingdom, don't brag about how many people you have in the building.

Verses 18 – 19, *I'm bold enough to tell you only what CHRIST has done through me to bring people who are not Jewish to obedience. By what I have said and done, by the power of miraculous and amazing signs, and by the power of GOD's Spirit, I have finished spreading the Good News about CHRIST from Jerusalem to Illyricum.*

I think that's the problem. People need to stop bragging and start serving. If you're not serving, Paul says then you don't have the right to brag! Paul blows me away in verse 20. I think this is what the Church is doing nowadays. *My goal was to spread the Good News where the name of CHRIST was not known. I didn't want to build on a foundation which others had laid.* Wow!

Watch this. Paul said, "I preach CHRIST where His name was not known." The problem in the Church is, that we keep preaching CHRIST to each other. That's why churches are swapping members. The Church is not taking the Good News about CHRIST to people that need it.

Yes, I believe in finding a church where the Word is going forth. I also believe people should be coming to the Church to get delivered. When someone accepts CHRIST, we should rejoice. Someone accepting CHRIST is more important than someone joining a church. Swapping members is nothing to brag about. People getting delivered is something to rejoice about.

Look at what Paul says happens when someone accepts CHRIST in verse 21. *As Scripture says, "Those who were never told about Him will see, and those who never heard will understand."* If somebody accepts CHRIST at our ministry, Divine Deliverance Ministries, and then that person goes to another church and joins over there, look at what Paul says in verse 20, "That pastor is only building on what I have already established." Paul said in verse 20, I don't want to build on a foundation which others had laid. Paul said, "I want to conquer new territory. I want to build the Kingdom and not rearrange the Kingdom."

Remember how Paul wanted to desperately visit the Roman Christians in Rome? He wanted to fellowship with them. He heard about how the message of CHRIST was spreading all over Rome. He was pleased with the work that was taken place in Rome. Verses 22 – 23, *This is what has so often kept me from visiting you. But now I have no new opportunities for work in this region. For many years I have wanted to visit you.* In other words, Paul said, "As much as I want to meet you, I'm out here laboring trying to bring people to CHRIST. It doesn't do me any good to come witness
in Rome. I'll just be witnessing to Believers." We're not supposed to witness to each other. We are supposed to strengthen each other in the faith.

Paul says, "My purpose when I come to Rome is not to witness to the saints, but to fellowship with the saints. Not to reshuffle the saints, but to take care of business by fellowshipping and helping strengthen the saints."

What was Paul's purpose for wanting to come to Rome, then? Look at verse 24. *Now I am on my way to Spain, so I hope to see you when I come your way. After I have enjoyed your company for a while, I hope that you will support my trip to Spain.* His purpose for visiting them was to fellowship and take up an offering. Uh oh! Please don't stop reading. Let's get a clear understanding of Paul's purpose. His purpose wasn't to drive a fancy car or wear fancy clothes. His purpose was to further the ministry. His purpose for wanting to visit the Christians in Rome was not to witness to those that were already saved, but to fellowship with the saints and to take care of business.

Enough people are witnessing to people who are already saved. We need to be taking the message of JESUS CHRIST around the world to people who are not saved. We need to be laying new foundations! Every time we lay a new foundation, and every time someone accepts CHRIST, it increases the Kingdom. GOD doesn't want us swapping members. HE wants us to increase the Kingdom.

Verses 25 – 29, *Right now I'm going to Jerusalem to bring help to the Christians there. Because the Believers in Macedonia and Greece owe a debt to the Christians in Jerusalem, they have decided to take up a collection for the poor among the Christians in Jerusalem. These Macedonians and Greeks have shared the spiritual wealth of the Christians in Jerusalem. So they are obligated to use their earthly wealth to help them. When the collection is completed and I have officially turned the money over to the Christians in Jerusalem, I will visit you on my way to Spain. I know that when I come to you I will bring the full blessing of CHRIST.*

Paul is taking up an offering to help the struggling Believers in Jerusalem and to support his mission in Spain. His main focus was supporting the

Believers who were in need. What has Paul been teaching us in the last few chapters? It's the job of those who are strong in the faith to *bear the infirmities of those that are weak.*

Paul didn't just talk the talk. We see him taking his advice. The reason churches nowadays will not help struggling churches is that every church is competing with one another. If we start focusing on building the Kingdom instead of our individual churches, then the Kingdom will grow by leaps and bounds. But as long as the Church keeps competing against each other, as long as, "I have more members than you, then I'm okay," the Kingdom will never grow. We are too busy competing against one another, instead of us going out and making new disciples for the Kingdom. We are more focused on stealing other people's members who should already be saved.

To create new disciples, means I have to get out in the vineyard and labor. To steal other people's members and build my building by swapping members, then I don't have to focus on doing effective ministry. All I have to do is concentrate on gimmicks that will bring people from other ministries to my building. If you have to result to gimmicks to build your ministry, then it's going to take gimmicks to keep your ministry.

The danger of resulting in gimmicks are, that you don't create an atmosphere that will bring deliverance. You just have to create a show that will keep people's attention. GOD is not a part of the production. HE is more attracted to an atmosphere where people are being delivered, to people who are trying to be set free, those who want to get healed, and where people want to experience HIS presence and not come to be entertained. GOD is not trying to entertain us. HE is more concerned about changing us. People nowadays sit in church waiting to be entertained.

Verse 30, *Brothers and sisters, I encourage you through our Lord JESUS CHRIST and by the love that the Spirit creates, to join me in my struggle. Pray to GOD for me.* Look at what Paul is asking the Believers. He tells the Believers to join him in his struggle and to pray for him in his struggle. To labor with him in his struggle. Effective ministry is not easy. To do effective ministry is a lot harder than putting on a production. Trying to deliver someone out of their sins is a lot harder than trying to entertain someone.

To entertain someone, you just need to find out the latest trend; what's popular, and what's popping. To deliver someone, you have to tell them what they don't want to hear, which is not popping or popular. However, it will save their life. If you want to fill all the seats, make your service popping. If you want a standing room only. Do what is popular. Paul didn't tell the Believers, "Let's do what will get everyone's attention." Paul tells these Believers to join him in the struggle. The good news is, that the struggle is rewarding.

That's why people choose not to attend Bible study. It's a struggle. That's why ministries that refuse to compromise GOD's Word are not packed out on Sundays. To live right and holy can be a struggle.

To prove to you that people are more attracted to what's popular, have you ever noticed, that when people put up videos of their church service, most time it's not of the Pastor's message? It's when the people start shouting. The shouting part is the entertaining part. The message part is the life-changing part. You shouldn't do the shouting part until you hear the message part.

After Paul tells the Believers to pray for him and to join him in the struggle, look at what he says in verse 31. "Pray for me" *that I will be rescued from those people in Judea who refuse to believe. Pray that GOD's people in Jerusalem will accept the help I bring.* Paul says, "Pray for me that I will be rescued from those who refuse to believe what I am preaching."

Ministry is like a battleground. Most people don't want to hear what GOD has to say. Here's what we do nowadays. Instead of us gearing up and going out on the battlefield to do effective ministry, we would rather compromise GOD's Word and make it entertaining so ministry won't be a struggle.

That's why Paul tells Timothy in 1st Timothy 6:12 to *fight the good fight of faith*. Know that it's going to be a fight. Paul says, "Don't worry about the fight. Even though it's going to be a fight. It's a good fight." You might have to fight to get someone delivered. If they get delivered from the fight, it was a good fight. You might have to struggle to get someone saved. If that person becomes saved, it was a good fight. You might have to labor to get someone set free. Don't worry about the fight. It's a good fight.

Believers nowadays are running from the fight. Even though Paul said it's a good fight. Believers are running from the struggle. Even though it's a good struggle.

Ministry nowadays mindset is, "If it's a struggle, I'm not fighting. If ministry is not convenient, then I'm not showing up!" So now, the ministry has to turn into production to get people to show up. It has to have fancy lighting. The choir has to be on point. The music has to be just right. Let's not talk about ministry in Los Angeles. People are attracted to celebrities. There's only ONE celebrity in the Kingdom. HE alone is worthy of our praise. HE alone should be the only one receiving all the glory.

Everybody wants to know, "When is it going to be my time? When are they going to sing my song? When is Pastor going to allow me to preach?" The problem with ministry today is, that we can't find anyone to be faithful. Most people are too busy trying to be famous! Everybody wants to have their moment to shine, while the Word of GOD is being neglected. How about, we let it be your turn, once you have come in from laboring. We'll let it be your turn once you have endured the struggle.

To show you that effective ministry is a struggle, look at what Paul says in verses 32 – 33. *Also, pray that by the will of GOD I may come to you with joy and be refreshed when I am with you. May the GOD of peace be with you all. Amen.* Paul says, "When I come to you, I'm coming to you to get refreshed." Watch this, "From my laboring." Notice what he says in verse

32. He says, "So, we can be refreshed together." In other words, hopefully, after all of us have labored and struggled to preach this Gospel to a world that needs it, we can come together and encourage each other. Hopefully, we can come together and talk about how many people were added to the Kingdom and not brag about how many people joined our churches from other ministries. Hopefully, we can talk about what we did for GOD.

2nd Corinthians 5:9 (NIV) says *So we make it our goal to please HIM, whether we are at home, in the body, or away from it.* Only what we do for CHRIST will last!

Chapter 16
Paul's Farewell

A lot of people don't preach or teach from chapter 16. It seems to be nothing but a list of names that may or may not be important. These names are mentioned, because either they were personal friends of Paul who lived in Rome, or they were with him in the city of Corinth and now are residing in the city of Rome. We won't deal with all of the twenty-six individuals and their contributions to the church. However, isn't it remarkable how in chapter 15 Paul just talked about CHRIST giving us the right to talk about what we do for GOD. Then right here in chapter 16, out of all of these twenty-six names that Paul mentions, Paul doesn't talk about what position they held. He doesn't deal with what their title was. He recognizes them based on their willingness to serve. As disciples, GOD calls all of us to serve. If your position is not bringing anyone into the Kingdom, you have nothing to brag about anyway.

After Paul mentions those who were serving, look what Paul says in verse 17. *Brothers and sisters, I urge you to watch out for those people who create divisions and who make others fall away from the Christian faith by teaching doctrine that is not the same as you have learned. Stay away from them.* Wow! That was kind of clever how Paul did that. He just gave us twenty-six names of people who were willing to serve. Right after he introduces those who were willing to serve, he tells the Believers in Rome to *watch out for those who create divisions* by teaching false doctrine.

Understand the correlation. Paul says they will come in bragging about their titles while causing division. You will know those who are up to no good; even though they carry a title, they are not willing to serve. You have to be very careful about people who are more concerned about showing up when it's 'lights, camera, action' than they are about showing up to serve. My question is, if you're not willing to serve, then why are you showing up?

Paul says in verse 17, "*Watch* out for them. They will create division. They don't know how to serve. But, you better believe they know how to create division." Look at what Paul continues to say. Not only will they create division, but they will also cause others to fall away from the faith. Anyone that drives more people away from ministry than they draw people to ministry is exactly who Paul is talking about. He warns the Believers to *watch* out for them. Not only does he warns us to *watch* out for them, but he says to *stay away from them*.

Verse 18, *People like these are not serving CHRIST our Lord. They are serving their own desires. By their smooth talk and flattering words, they deceive unsuspecting people.* Paul says these people are not serving CHRIST. They're just looking for opportunities to divide the church. Why? Because they serve their desires. Watch this, they're not interested in growing the Kingdom. They're too busy trying to push their own agendas. They *are serving their own desires*. Their agendas divide the Kingdom, because they desire to destroy the Church. Paul warns us to not only watch out for them, but to *stay away from them* as well.

The keyword in verse 17 is *watch*. The reason Paul tells us we have to *watch* is that they will be good at blending in. You can always tell who they are. They're not willing to serve, have their false doctrine, and they cause division within the ministry. The danger of not recognizing them is, that by the time you recognize who they are, they have already caused division. They have already run people away. Paul said in verse 18, they don't come to serve CHRIST. They come to deceive the Believers; they have their own desires.

What Paul is saying is, "True Believers, have to be proven." Look at what he says in verse 18. He says People like these do not serve CHRIST. Anyone that's not willing to serve needs to be watched. If you are a Believer and you're not willing to serve, then, what's your agenda? If you don't come to help, you must come to hinder. If you're not willing to build, your agenda must be to *destroy*.

Paul tells the Roman Christians, "I have given you a list of Believers you can trust." If anyone other than them decides to pop their head up, watch'em!

First, see if they're willing to serve. Then, see what they truly believe. Next, see what matters to them the most. If they're more concerned about their stuff than they are about GOD's stuff, then *stay away from them*. Their desires will cause division in the Church. Paul says, "Mark'em, then avoid'em." In other words, identify who they are and *stay away from them*.

Verse 19, *Everyone has heard about your obedience and this makes me happy for you. I want you to do what is good and to avoid what is evil.* Paul is telling the Believers to stay on the right course. Don't allow the popularity of what you're doing *good* go to your head and cause you to do *evil*. Just because everyone is talking about how well you guys are doing, continue to do *good*. He says be wise in what's *good*. Continue to use wisdom.

If you continue to use wisdom to do *good*, look at what Paul says in verse 20. *The GOD of peace will quickly crush Satan under your feet. May the goodwill of our Lord JESUS be with you!* Paul says, all we have to do is concentrate on doing what's right, and GOD will take care of the rest. You don't have to worry about what the devil is planning, as long as you concentrate on doing what's right. Verse 20 lets us know GOD will crush the devil's plans.

When we don't get caught up in the accolades of the people, but we are wise about doing what's right, *The GOD of peace will quickly crush Satan under your feet.* As long as we are doing what's right, GOD will keep Satan under our feet. As long as we are watchful and focused on making *good* decisions, GOD will keep Satan under our feet. If you want Satan to stay under your feet, you have to keep serving while being watchful and be wise in what is good. Paul says the grace of our Lord JESUS CHRIST *be with you*. Amen. In other words, "I'm praying for you that you continue to serve, be watchful, and stay focused on making good decisions." I'm praying for you.

After Paul sends greetings from all those that were serving with him in verses 21 – 24, he then gives the benediction in verses 25 – 27. *GOD can strengthen you by the Good News and the message I tell about JESUS CHRIST. He can strengthen you by revealing the mystery that was kept in silence for a very long time but now is publicly known. The everlasting GOD ordered that what the prophets wrote must be shown to the people of every nation to bring them to the obedience that is associated with faith. GOD alone is wise. Glory belongs to him through JESUS CHRIST forever! Amen.*

NOTES

Annistonstar.com. (2022). PASTOR CHIP THORNTON: Don't stoop to be a king (column). Retrieved from https://www.annistonstar.com/the_st_clair_times/stclair_religion/pastor-chip-thornton-don-t-stoop-to-be-a-king-column/article_c12b5bc2-f989-11e8-aeea-13443f1eccbc.html

www.ingramcontent.com/pod-product-compliance
Lightning Source LLC
Chambersburg PA
CBHW051433290426
44109CB00016B/1533